QUIZ ENCOUNTERS OF THE TRIVIA KIND

Chris Smart & Mike Lewis

Thank you for purchasing this quiz book. We know there are many options available in the market.

Quiz Encounters Of The Trivia Kind contains around 180 quiz rounds.

Most of the questions in the book have been used by us to entertain many quizzers - so they are proven to be successful! This book will provide entertainment for individuals, for family and friends, for social gatherings or part of bigger quiz events. Each quiz has the answers shown on the following page.

ABOUT THE AUTHORS

Mike Lewis is the lead writer and presenter of The Inquizitors, a professional quiz outfit who have presented quizzes for numerous corporate and charity events throughout the UK since 1989. He has been writing quizzes for even more years.

Mike is now retired and lives in Olveston, just outside his home city of Bristol. He is a former marketing & commercial executive who worked within professional football for over 30 years. Mike also ran businesses in retail and marketing.

To Rob and Mo, my fellow Inquizitors, I couldn't have done it without you.

Chris Smart also lives in Olveston, having been brought up in South Gloucestershire. Now retired, Chris spent 42 years in the Water Industry. He enjoys local sports, skittles and dog walking.

Chris has been involved with Quizzing for about 40 years and was a winner on Radio 1 Treble Top Darts theme quiz. He has compiled and run quizzes for pubs and local organisations for 30 years.

To Will our proud, loving and faithful friend, ... always in our hearts.

INDEX

INDEX

THE LAST SHALL BE FIRST

The last letter of the first answer will be the first letter of the next answer and so on. Finally the last letter of answer 10 is the first letter of the first answer!

1. What word is a foxes home and the 5th largest planet in the Solar System?
2. By what name is a large Spanish estate with a dwelling known?
3. What name is given to a robot made in human likeness?
4. Mainly in Bristol and the West Country, what name is given to the footwear Plimsolls?
5. In the John Le Carre novel *Tinker, Tailor, Soldier, Spy*, what was the surname of the central intelligence character?
6. In 1896 which Canadian Territory did the Klondike Gold Rush originate?
7. Which chemical symbol is Ni?
8. Clamping, Cradling and Scooping are terms used in which sport?
9. What name is used to describe a large retail store that sells a wide variety of goods?
10. Which soul singer was shot dead by his father a day before his 45th birthday in 1984?

TEN SHADES OF BLUE

All answers contain a variation of blue

1. What is the national flower of Germany?
2. Which ship was found abandoned and adrift in the Atlantic in 1872?
3. Keble & Oriel are colleges at which university?
4. What type of atomic weapon was designed to produce more radiation than blast?
5. Name the Cluedo character, Elizabeth, Lady of Arlington Grange.
6. Name the Northern Premier League club based in Crosby, Liverpool.
7. Which song by The Village People reached No 2 in 1979?
8. Name the dye famously used by the warrior queen Boudicca?
9. David McCallum and Joanna Lumley starred in which TV series that ran from 1979/82?
10. Name the UK's largest Pay-TV broadcaster, owned by Comcast.

THE LAST SHALL BE FIRST ANSWERS

1. EARTH
2. HACIENDA
3. ANDROID
4. DAPS
5. SMILEY
6. YUKON
7. NICKEL
8. LACROSSE
9. EMPORIUM
10. MARVIN GAYE

Answer 1

TEN SHADES OF BLUE ANSWERS

1. CORNFLOWER
2. MARY CELESTE {MINERAL)
3. OXFORD
4. COBALT BOMB
5. MRS PEACOCK
6. MARINE
7. IN THE NAVY
8. WOAD
9. SAPPHIRE & STEEL
10. SKY

Answer 2

CONNECTIONS (1)

All the correct answers are connected. Find the connection

1. Which 1970s/1980s rock band was made up of Gordon Sumner, Andy Summers, Stewart Copeland and, briefly, Henry Padovani?

2. A long-running US TV show (1994 - 2004), featured a Green, a Buffay, 2 Gellers,a Tribbiani and a Bing, whose middle name was Muriel. But what was the first name of the latter?

3. Sagittarius serpentarius is the formal name of which sub-Saharan bird?

4. Which band, formed by two ex-Bay City Rollers, had a 1975 Number 1 hit in the UK, Germany and Australia with 'January'?

5. Originally auditioning for the role of Hilda Ogden, which *Coronation Street* actress plays a barmaid who is believed to have served more than 200,000 portions of her Hot Pot?

6. Who was shot and killed during a protest in London's St James' Square in April 1984?

7. Which 1931-born Texan jockey won 11 US Triple Crown races and was ironically crippled in 1991after a car crash in a Ford Bronco?

8. In 1925, Alfred Roberts, a Lincolnshire grocer, and his wife, Ethel, had a second daughter. How did she become better known?

9. Which 1970s Northern variety show, compered by Colin Crompton, introduced Cannon & Ball, Paul Daniels and The Grumbleweeds?

10. Willy Loman was the lead character in which Arthur Miller play (1949)?

MUSIC EXTENDED ROUND (1)

An extended round is great to add variety to a quiz night. Sheets are handed out at the beginning of the quiz and answers have to be completed at a later stage of the quiz - quite often the half-time break. Often this takes the form of a Picture Round. However there are other options. This round is a simple job of listing as many nominated hits as you can within a specified time. See the instruction below. The complete list of possible answers is shown on the following page.

*Name as many of the Top 10 Hits of **WESTLIFE** as you can in 10 minutes!*

CONNECTIONS (1) ANSWERS

1. THE POLICE

2. CHANDLER

3. SECRETARY BIRD

4. PILOT

5. BETTY DRIVER *(PLAYED BETTY TURPIN)*

6. WPC YVONNE FLETCHER

7. WILLIE SHOEMAKER

8. BARONESS MARGARET THATCHER

9. THE WHEELTAPPERS AND SHUNTERS CLUB

10. DEATH OF A SALESMAN

CONNECTION: ALL OCCUPATIONS

MUSIC EXTENDED ROUND (1) ANSWERS
WESTLIFE TOP 10 HITS

AMAZING
BETTER MAN
BOP BOP BABY
FLYING WITHOUT WINGS
FOOL AGAIN
HELLO MY LOVE
HEY WHATEVER
HOME
I HAVE A DREAM / SEASONS IN THE SUN
IF I LET YOU GO
LIGHTHOUSE
MANDY
MISS YOU NIGHTS
MY LOVE
OBVIOUS
QUEEN OF MY HEART
THE ROSE
SAFE
SWEAR IT AGAIN
TONIGHT
UNBREAKABLE
UP AGAINST THE WORLD
UPTOWN GIRL
WHAT ABOUT NOW
WHAT MAKES A MAN
WHEN YOU TELL ME THAT YOU LOVE ME (feat Diana Ross)
WORLD OF OUR OWN
YOU RAISE ME UP

THE CORRECT SEQUENCE

Put each of the following in the right order

1. Continents: put these in order of size, largest to smallest. Europe - Africa - Asia

2. Oceans: put these in order of size, largest to smallest. Pacific - Atlantic - Indian

3. Islands: put these in order of size, largest to smallest. Great Britain - Greenland - Cuba

4. Desserts: put these in order of size, largest to smallest. Arabian - Gobi - Sahara

5. Rivers put these in order of size, longest first. Yangtze (Chang Jiang) - Amazon - Mississippi (Missouri - Jefferson)

6. Planets: put these in order of size, largest to smallest. Mercury - Neptune - Jupiter

7. Towers: put these in order of height, tallest first. Bank of China (Hong Kong) - Empire State Building (NY) - The Shard (London)

8. Kings of England: put these in date order of earliest first. Charles I - Henry I - George I

9. Famous painters born. Earliest to latest. Claude Monet - Leonardo da Vinci - Rembrandt

10. Composers: put these in date order of earliest first. Vivaldi - Strauss - Beethoven

COUNTING ONE TO TEN

The answers are 1,2,3,4,5,6,7,8,9 or 10 - but not in that order!

1. What was the number of the last unmanned Apollo spacecraft to be launched?

2. In Genesis 7:2, (King James Bible), how many pairs of clean animals and birds does God tell Noah to take on to the ark?

3. What number shirt did Nobby Stiles wear in the 1966 World Cup Final?

4. How many UK No 1 hits did both the Rolling Stones and Oasis notch up (as 1/2020)?

5. What wind force number is 'Light Air' on the Beaufort wind force scale?

6. Name the 1979 Blake Edwards rom-com starring Julie Andrews and Dudley Moore.

7. A penalty or drop goal is worth this number of points in Rugby Union.

8. Mars has how many moons?

9. How many major gods and goddesses are there in Egyptian mythology?

10. How many pillars make up the basic rules of Islam that all Muslims should follow?

THE CORRECT SEQUENCE ANSWERS

1. ASIA, AFRICA, EUROPE

2. PACIFIC, ATLANTIC, INDIAN

Answer 3

3. GREENLAND, GB, CUBA

4. SAHARA, ARABIAN, GOBI

5. AMAZON, MISSISSIPPI (MISSOURI JEFFERSON), YANGTZE

6. JUPITER, NEPTUNE, MERCURY

7. BANK OF CHINA (386M), EMPIRE STATE BUILDING (381M), THE SHARD (310M)

8. HENRY I (1100 - 35), CHARLES I (1625 - 49), GEORGE I (1714 - 27)

9. LEONARDO DIVINCI (B1452), REMBRANDT (B 1606), CLAUDE MONET (B 1840)

10. VIVALDI (B 1678), BEETHOVEN (B 1770), STRAUSS (B 1864)

COUNTING ONE TO TEN ANSWERS

1. APOLLO **6**

2. 'EVERY CLEAN ANIMAL BY **7**

Answer 3

3. NOBBY STILES WORE NUMBER **4**

4. ROLLING STONES AND OASIS HAVE HAD **8** NUMBER ONES

5. BEAUFORT SCALE **1**

6. BLAKE EDWARDS FILM IS **10**

7. A DROP GOAL IS **3** POINTS

8. MARS HAS **2** MOONS

9. THERE ARE **9** EGYPTIAN GODS AND GODDESSES

10. THERE ARE **5** PILLARS OF ISLAM

E.......E BY GUM!

Every answer begins and ends with the letter E

1.HIS MOST FAMOUS ALTER EGO.

2. WHICH NORTH UK TEAM WEARS THIS KIT?

3.WHICH PIER WENT UP IN SMOKE IN 2014?

4.YOUR STARTER!

5.A WRITER OF MYSTERY & MACABRE

6.NEST OF AN EAGLE

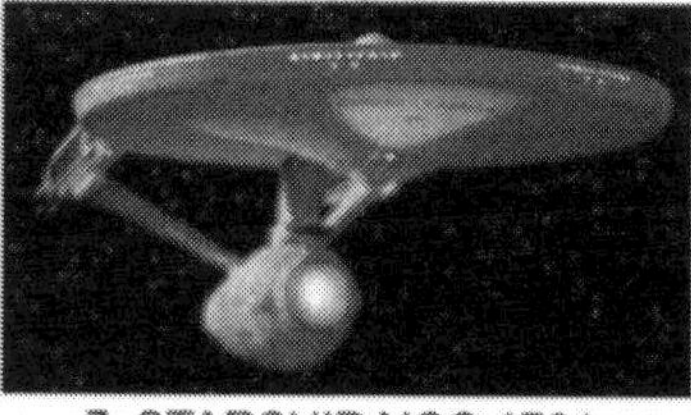

7 .STARSHIP NCC-1701

8.SEASIDE MANAGER

9.ACADEMY AWARD WINNING ACTOR

10. SINGER AND FICTIONAL CHARACTER SHARE A NAME

FILM ANAGRAMS

Solve these to find well-known movies

1. CHOPSY (5) 2. LONG FRIDGE (10) 3. THE DEATH FROG (3,9)
4. IN ATTIC (7) 5. OH ONE MALE (4,5)

E....E BY GUM! ANSWERS

1. EDNA EVERAGE
2. EAST FIFE
3. EASTBOURNE
4. EGG MAYONNAISE
5. EDGAR ALLAN POE
6. EYRIE
7. ENTERPRISE
8. EDDIE HOWE
9. EDDIE REDMAYNE
10. ELIZA DOOLITTLE

FILM ANAGRAMS ANSWERS

1. PSYCHO

2. GOLDFINGER
3. THE GODFATHER
4. TITANIC
5. HOME ALONE

SOMETHING IN COMMON

Find the link

1. What do Football, Woolworth, Heinz and Dr Pepper have in common?
2. What do Karl Marx, Michael Faraday, Herbert Spencer and George Eliot have in common?
3. What do Romney Marsh, Suffolk, Clun, Forest and Swaledale have in common?
4. What do tulip, balloon, and flute have in common?
5. What did the poets Wordsworth, Tennyson, Masefield and Betjeman have in common?
6. What do nitrous oxide, sodium pentothal and cyclo propane have in common?
7. What do Micmac, Cree and Ojibwa have in common?
8. What do Coburg, Vienna, Cottage and Bloomer have in common?
9. Clout, Lost Head, Box and French are all types of what?
10. What links the 4 pictures below?

TRUE OR FALSE?

1. Ancient Egyptians placed their hands on onions when taking oaths?
2. The White House, Washington has 2,000 rooms?
3. Friday the 13th's occur whenever a month begins with a Sunday?
4. M&M stands for Mars and Moordale?
5. Australia is wider than the moon?
6. Letters in Braille are referred to as cells?
7. You share your birthday with over 15 million people worldwide?
8. Robert Wrigley created the first chewing gum?
9. There are two parts of the body that can't heal themselves?
10. The Great Wall of China is longer than the distance between London and Beijing?

SOMETHING IN COMMON ANSWERS

1. STUD POKER GAMES
2. ALL BURIED AT HIGHGATE CEMETERY
3. BREEDS OF SHEEP
4. TYPES OF WINE GLASS
5. POETS LAUREATE
6. GENERAL ANAESTHETICS
7. NORTH AMERICAN TRIBES
8. TYPES OF LOAF
9. TYPES OF NAIL
10. PREMIER LEAGUE NICKNAMES (AS AT 2019/20) *(FOXES, BLADES, WOLVES, TOFFEES)*

TRUE OR FALSE ANSWERS

1. TRUE. The onion symbolized eternity to the Egyptians

2. FALSE. 132 rooms, 35 bathrooms

3. TRUE. Fear of this date is friggatriskaidekaphobia or paraskevidekatriaphobia!

4. FALSE. M&M stands for Mars and Murrie

5. TRUE. Moon 3400km in diameter Australia almost 4000km

6. TRUE. 64 combinations are possible using one or more of six dots.

7. TRUE. Somewhere around 20.8 million!

8. FALSE. Thomas Adams is regarded as a founder of the chewing gum industry.

9. FALSE. There Is only one: the teeth

10. TRUE. London to Beijing is 8,136 km, Great Wall of China is 21,196.18 km

TOM HANKS MOVIES

1. In the movie *Sully*, Hanks plays a pilot, Captain Chesley Sullenberger who makes an emergency landing in which river?

2. Tom won back to back Oscars for Best Actor in 1993/4. Who previously achieved that feat?

3. In *Cast Away*, Hanks is marooned on an uninhabited island after his plane crashes in the South Pacific. Who is his employer?

4. Name the character played by Hanks in *Saving Private Ryan*.

5. Who was the female co-star in *Sleepless in Seattle* ?

6. Name the 1994 romantic comedy drama film based on the 1986 novel by Winston Groom.

7. Many movies have been based on Stephen King stories, but which is the highest grossing?

8. Which Hanks film sees a 12 year old boy putting a coin into an unusual antique arcade fortune teller machine called Zoltar Speaks?

9. Hanks is the voice of Woody in *Toy Story*. Who is the voice of Buzz Lightyear?

10. Hanks starred in *The DaVinci Code* in 2006. Who wrote the novel?

MIXED BAG

1. Who was responsible for losing Barings Bank £830 million in 1995?

2. How many different value coins are in circulation in the UK and what is their total value?

3. How many spikes on the Statue of Liberty's crown ?

4. Which dolls were not bought but 'adopted'?

5. How many murders are committed in the Hitchcock thriller *Psycho*?

6. What Australian landmark is nicknamed 'The Coathanger'?

7. In which country did Balti cooking originate?

8. Leap of the hare, tree climber, spinning top and chasing the sparrow are all positions described in detail in which book?

9. How many boys names feature in the NATO phonetic alphabet?

10. Missing vowels! Look at the phrase below and find a question that waiter may ask you?

WL DYL KT STHD SSR TMN

TOM HANKS MOVIES ANSWERS

1. THE HUDSON RIVER (NEW YORK)

2. SPENCER TRACY

Answer4

3. FED-EX

4. CAPTAIN JOHN MILLER

5. MEG RYAN

6. FORREST GUMP

7. THE GREEN MILE

8. BIG

9. TIM ALLEN

10. DAN BROWN

MIXED BAG ANSWERS

1. NICK LEESON

2. 8 (£3.88)

3. 7

4. CABBAGE PATCH DOLLS

Answer 4

5. JUST 2

6. SYDNEY HARBOUR BRIDGE

7. UNITED KINGDOM

8. THE KAMA SUTRA

9. 5 (Charlie, Mike, Oscar, Romeo, Victor)

10. WOULD YOU LIKE TO SEE THE DESSERT MENU?

WHAT'S WHAT!

1. Molly the whistling ———was a great success at the Drury Lane Theatre in 1840:
   A) Mermaid B) Oyster C) Policeman D) Kettle

2. One ounce of cress boiled down will produce enough cyanide to kill:
   A) an adult B) a cat C) a deer D) 2 mice

3. In competition darts the average speed that a dart hits the board is:
   A) 20 mph B) 30 mph C) 40 mph D) 50 mph

4. In the 55 minute interview Diana, Princess of Wales, gave to Martin Bashir in 1995, how many times did she mention the name Charles?: A) 12 times B) 10 C) 6 D) 2

5. The 10 shilling note went out of circulation on: A)10 April 1981:
   B) 20 November 1970 C) 1 April 1978 D) 8 November 1987

6. Giraffes cannot swim or —: A) cough B) jump C) sleep D) kneel

7. In Mongolia a traditional hangover cure is to eat what in a glass of tomato juice?:
   A) goat's testicle B) monkey's tail C) sheep's eye D) owl's tongue

8. Hedonophobia is fear of: A) nudity B) marriage C) pleasure D) mushrooms

9. A survey in the Daily Telegraph in 2009 found the favourite 'smells' of Brits. What was voted the top smell?: A) fresh baked bread B) clean sheets C) mown grass D) fresh flowers

10. Frederick Sanger invented : A) Insulin B) Safety Pin C) Inflatable Life Raft D) Aspirin

POT POURRI

1. In which year did the Scots defeat the English at Bannockburn?

2. In a street of 100 consecutive numbered houses (1-100), how many No. 9's are used?

3. What cost 37p when it was abolished in 1988?

4. Adrenaline is produced by the adrenal glands located where in the body?

5. What type of car is associated with Lady Penelope Creighton-Ward?

6. What vegetable includes the varieties: Burplass Tasty Green;Tokyo Green, Slice King?

7. Where was the body of George Mallory found In 1999; 75 years after his death?

8. What links the death of Henry V with telephone caller identification?

9. What can go up a chimney down but not down a chimney up?

10. What connects these four pictures?

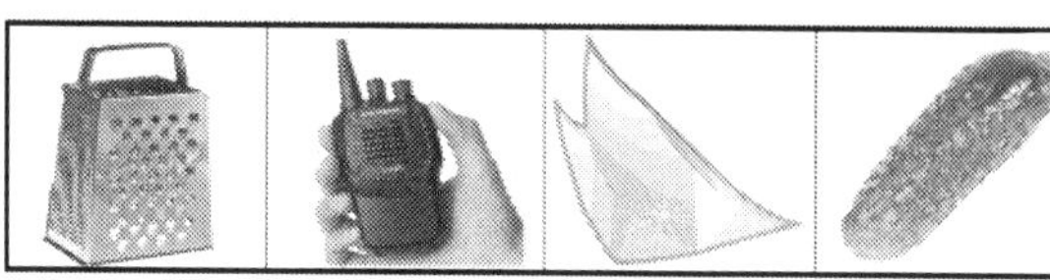

WHAT'S WHAT! ANSWERS

1. B) OYSTER

2. D) 2 MICE

3. C) 40 MPH

4. D) 2 TIMES

5. B) 20 NOVEMBER 1970

Answer 5

6. A) COUGH

7. C) SHEEP'S EYE

8. C) PLEASURE

9. A) FRESH BAKED BREAD

10. A) INSULIN

POT POURRI ANSWERS

1. 1314

2. 20

3. DOG LICENCE

4. ADJACENT TO THE KIDNEYS

5. (A PINK) ROLLS ROYCE (Lady Penelope)

6. CUCUMBER

7. MOUNT EVEREST

Answer 6

8. 1471

9. AN UMBRELLA

10. LONDON SKYCRAPERS

COGNITION

1. Which England Rugby Union International made his debut in 2012 and was made captain 6 years later when they played in France?

2. What is the only anagram of the word MONDAY?

3. What is the only fruit to have seeds on the outside?

4. What did US President Barack Obama promise his daughter during his victory speech?

5. Where did the Muffin Man live?

6. What did Edward Love invent: power steering, cat litter or air conditioning?

7. In the game Cluedo, which room can be accessed via the secret passage way from the study?

8. In which year was DNA discovered? A)1947 B)1953 C)1967 D)1983

9. On which day of the week was the 9/11 attack on the World Trade Center?

10. What should go in the 4th box?

1994: TORVILL & DEAN – OLYMPIC ICE DANCE COMPETITION	1995: PANORAMA SPECIAL – PRINCESS DIANA	1996: ONLY FOOLS AND HORSES CHRISTMAS SPECIAL PART 3	?

TAKING THE MICHAEL!

All answers have MICHAEL in them

1. Who the main protagonist of Mario Puzo's novel, *The Godfather*?

2. Who married baroness Marie-Christine Von Reibriz in 1978?

3. Who became leader of the Labour Party in 1980?

4. Which actor, whose films include *The Cider House Rules*, received a Knighthood in 2000?

5. Name the man who broke into Buckingham Palace and sat chatting to the Queen on her bed?

6. Who wrote the novel *The English Patient*?

7. Which singer was born Georgios Kyriacos Panayiotou in 1963?

8. Which member of The Goons was born in 1921 and died in 1996?

9. Which son of a former footballer went on to score 40 goals for England and captain the national team?

10. Which actor got a BAFTA award for portraying *The Singing Detective* on TV and knighted in 1998?

COGNITION ANSWERS

1. OWEN FARRELL

Answer 1

2. DYNAMO

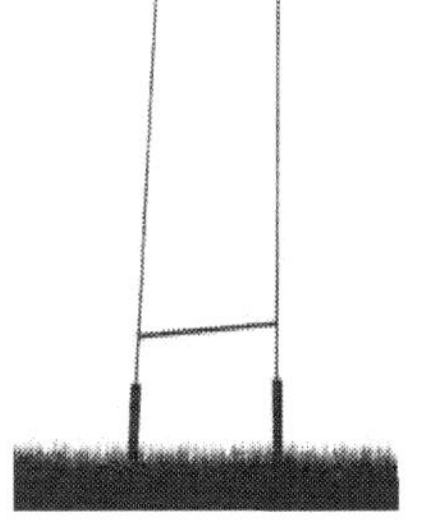

3. STRAWBERRY

4. A PUPPY

5. IN DRURY LANE

6. CAT LITTER

7. THE KITCHEN

8. B) 1953

9. TUESDAY

10. 1997: FUNERAL OF DIANA, PRINCESS OF WALES
Most watched TV programmes by year

TAKING THE MICHAEL ANSWERS

1. MICHAEL CORLEONE

2. PRINCE MICHAEL OF KENT

3. MICHAEL FOOT

4. SIR MICHAEL CAINE

5. MICHAEL FAGAN

6. MICHAEL ONDAATJE

7. GEORGE MICHAEL

8. MICHAEL BENTINE

9. MICHAEL OWEN

10. SIR MICHAEL GAMBON

BIRDS OF A FEATHER

All answers contain the name of a bird

1. Which famous architect designed St Paul's Cathedral?

2. What was the title of the instrumental by Fleetwood Mac that reached number one in 1968?

3. What were the first four words broadcast from the surface of the moon on 20 July 1969?

4. Which Falkland Islands' airstrip was recaptured on 28 May 1982 during the conflict with Argentina?

5. In which country could you see the ruins of ancient city Ephesus?

6. Which 800 feet high building in London's Docklands was designed by Cesar Pelli?

7. What is the type name of domesticated fowl, a subspecies of the red junglefowl (Gallus gallus)?

8. Which town in South Bedfordshire stands at the north eastern end of the Vale of Aylesbury?

9. What was the name of Sleepy Hollow's schoolmaster in stories by Washington Irving?

10. Who went to sea in a beautiful pea green boat?

FOLLOW ON (1)

The last letter of the 1st answer is the 1st letter of the next answer on to Question 10

1. Montevideo is the capital of which South American country?

2. What name is the outer parts of a ship's square mast rigging, from which sailors were often hung in olden days?

3. What name is given to the implement used in croquet to strike the ball?

4. What was the name of the character played by the late Roger Lloyd-Pack in *Only Fools and Horses*?

5. Which present day news agency was named after a German industrialist who began with a telegraph company?

6. Which member of Girls Aloud briefly appeared in Coronation Street in 2015 and won Celebrity Big Brother 20 in 2017?

7. By what name, of French origin, are small strips of chicken coated with breadcrumbs and deep fried?

8. How would a married woman be formally addressed in Spanish?

9. What is the common name for the popular houseplant St Paulia?

10. What surname connects the inventor of a sub-machine gun and a British Olympic decathlon champion in 1980 and 1984?

BIRDS OF A FEATHER ANSWERS

1. SIR CHRISTOPHER WREN
2. ALBATROSS
3. THE EAGLE HAS LANDED
4. GOOSE GREEN
5. TURKEY
6. CANARY WHARF TOWER
7. CHICKEN
8. LEIGHTON BUZZARD
9. ICHABOD CRANE
10. THE OWL AND THE PUSSYCAT

FOLLOW ON (1) ANSWERS

1. URUGUAY
2. YARDARM
3. MALLET
4. TRIGGER

5. REUTERS
6. SARAH HARDING
7. GOUJONS
8. SENORA
9. AFRICAN VIOLET
10. THOMPSON

CHILDREN'S CHARACTERS AND WORK

Write the occupations of these fictional characters from film and TV

1. PAT CLIFTON
2. MISS HOOLIE
3. LIZZIE SPARKES
4. BUNSEN HONEYDEW
5. MR RUSTY
6. HENRY BROWN
7. RITA SKEETER
8. CHIPPY & NIBS MINTON
9. MICKEY MURPHY
10. SIR TOPHAM HATT

THIS AND THAT

General Knowledge Questions

1. Which Gloucestershire town was known in Roman Times as Corinium?

2. ***Lies down to act.*** Is an anagram of which famous actor?

3. Who replaced John Bercow as Speaker of the House of Commons in 2019?

4. Awarded 71 times since its inception in 1943 for outstanding acts of bravery or devotion to duty, who is eligible to be awarded the Dickin Medal?

5. How many eyes does a bee have?

6. From which song do these lyrics come . 'Golden days before they end. Whisper secrets to wind. Your baby won't be near you anymore….'?

7. Who was Australian Test cricket captain for the 2019 tour of England?

8. Which organisation was founded by The Rev Chad Varrah in 1953?

9. Who played the role of Miss Jones in the TV sit-com *Rising Damp*?

10. What is the link between the four locations below:

CORRACHADH MÒR	DUNNET HEAD	LOWESTOFT NESS	LIZARD POINT

CHILDREN'S CHARACTERS & WORK ANSWERS

Answer 1

1. POSTMAN (POSTMAN PAT)

2. NURSERY TEACHER (BALAMORY)

3. BAKER (CAMBERWICK GREEN)

4. SCIENTIST (THE MUPPET SHOW)

5. ROUNDABOUT OPERATOR (MAGIC ROUNDABOUT)

6. RISK ANALYST/INSURANCE SALESMAN (PADDINGTON)

7. NEWSPAPER REPORTER/JOURNALIST (HARRY POTTER)

8. CARPENTERS (TRUMPTON)

9. VET (FIREMAN SAM)

10. RAILWAY CONTROLLER (THOMAS THE TANK ENGINE)

THIS AND THAT ANSWERS

1. CIRENCESTER

2. CLINT EASTWOOD

3. LINDSAY HOYLE

4. ANIMALS ON ACTIVE DUTY

5. 5

6. IT'S OVER by ROY ORBISON

7. TIM PAINE

8. SAMARITANS

9. FRANCES DE LA TOUR.

10. EXTREME POINTS OF THE BRITISH MAINLAND - *W, N, E, S*

Answer 4

GENERAL TRIVIA

1. Which TV cook established the River Cottage series?
2. ANAGRAM: Song from a musical **TWO HEADED DOGS TEA** (8,5)
3. What is the Statue of Liberty holding in her left hand?
4. Which pop group did Zayn Malik leave in 2015?
5. What variety of cabbage shares its name with a hotel on The Strand in London?
6. What type of transport is a packet?
7. Who wrote the series of novels about Mary Poppins?
8. If you had committed Fratricide who would you have killed?
9. The term vulpine refers to which animals?
10. Look at the box below and state what should go in the 4th box.

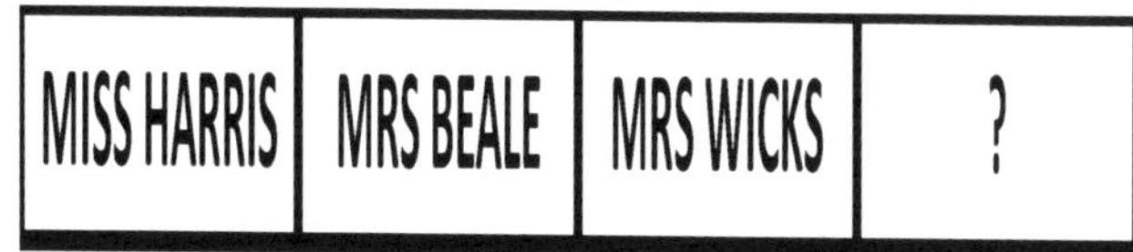

MISS HARRIS	MRS BEALE	MRS WICKS	?

BITS AND PIECES

1. Golden Knob and Tickled Pink are varieties of which fruit?
2. The Shining and Full Metal Jacket are films directed by whom?
3. What is the smallest British rodent?
4. According to the rhyme Solomon Grundy was born on a Monday, but on which day did he die?
5. Specifically, what part of your body is the Hallux?
6. Take Back Your Mink and Luck Be A Lady are songs from which musical?
7. By what name is a light midday lunch with tea derived in British India known?
8. What sporting event takes place annually at Prestbury Park?
9. Which son of Henry VIII and Jane Seymour was King of England between 1547 and 1553?
10. Which song contains these lyrics: *Maybe I didn't hold you all those lonely – lonely times And I guess I never told you. I'm so happy that you're mine If I make you feel second best, Girl I'm sorry I was blind.*

GENERAL TRIVIA ANSWERS

1. HUGH FEARNLEY WHITTINGSTALL.

2. THE DEADWOOD STAGE

3. A STONE TABLET

4. ONE DIRECTION

5. SAVOY

6. A BOAT

7. PL TRAVERS

8. YOUR BROTHER OR SISTER

9. FOXES

10. MRS BUTCHER
(The life of Pat from EastEnders)

BITS AND PIECES ANSWERS

1. APPLES

2. STANLEY KUBRICK

3. HARVEST MOUSE

4. SATURDAY

5. BIG TOE

6. GUYS AND DOLLS

7. TIFFIN

8. CHELTENHAM RACES (FEAT GOLD CUP)

9. EDWARD 6TH

10. ALWAYS ON MY MIND

LOGO MATCH

Whose logos are these?

NUMBER ONES OF THE 2010s

Who had the UK number one with the following songs?

1. *Bad Romance* 2. *Don't Wanna Go Home* 3. *Call My Name* 4. *Wake Me Up*

5. *All About that Bass* 6. *Sorry* 7. *7 Years* 8. *Look What You Made Me Do*

9. *In My Feelings* 10. *No Time To Die*

LOGO MATCH ANSWERS

1. PIZZA HUT
2. STARBUCKS
3. APPLE
4. MORRISONS
5. KELLOGGS
6. NEW BALANCE
7. PEPSI
8. HARIBO
9. MOVISTAR
10. BARCLAYS

Answer 2

NUMBER ONES OF THE 2010s ANSWERS

1. LADY GAGA
2. JASON DERULO
3. CHERYL
4. AVICII
5. MEGHAN TRAINOR
6. JUSTIN BIEBER
7. LUKAS GRAHAM
8. TAYLOR SWIFT
9. DRAKE
10. BILLIE ELISH

Answer 5

ANIMATED SCREEN ANIMALS

Character name and MovieTitle supplied. What type of animal was the character?

1. Lucifer. Cinderella
2. Bagheera. Jungle Book
3. Baloo. The Jungle Book
4. Snowball. The Secret Life of Pets
5. Dug. Up
6. Bartok. Anastasia
7. Flotsam & Jetsam. Little Mermaid
8. Remy. Ratatouille
9. Shifu. Kung Fu Panda
10. Flit. Pocahontas

CONNECTIONS (2)

Answer the first 9 questions and find the link using the answers for Q10

1. Name the 1971 film starring Gene Hackman and Roy Scheider, which concerns smuggling narcotics between Marseille and New York.
2. According to the Bible who was the first person to commit murder?
3. Which two men were responsible for writing and composing *HMS Pinafore*, *The Pirates of Penzance* and *The Mikado*?
4. Who is the British tennis player who won the men's singles at Wimbledon twice in the 21st century?
5. What Kurt Weill song, with lyrics by Bertolt Brecht, for their music drama *The Threepenny Opera* and was later a No 1 for Bobby Darin?
6. By what name is the pastime of skimming stones across a lake more commonly known?
7. What concrete structure was built in August 1961 and demolished in November 1989?
8. What was the British Army's standard rifle from its official adoption in 1895 until 1957?
9. Which river runs through the city of Chester and flows into the North Sea on the south side of the Wirral Peninsular?
10. And the connection between the answers?

ANIMATED SCREEN ANIMALS ANSWERS

1. CAT

2. PANTHER

3. BEAR

4. RABBIT

5. DOG

6. BAT

7. EELS

8. RAT

9. RED PANDA

10. HUMMINGBIRD

CONNECTIONS (2) ANSWERS

1. FRENCH CONNECTION – *DAWN FRENCH*
2. CAIN – *RUSSELL KANE*
3. GILBERT AND SULLIVAN – *RHOD GILBERT*
4. ANDY MURRAY – *AL MURRAY THE PUB LANDLORD*
5. MACK THE KNIFE – *LEE MACK*
6. DUCKS AND DRAKES - *CHARLIE DRAKE*

7. BERLIN WALL - *MAX WALL*
8. LEE ENFIELD - *HARRY ENFIELD*
9. THE RIVER DEE – *JACK DEE*
10. COMEDIANS

GOING UP!

Multi choice questions with an increasing value

1. During WWII the Nazis tried to assassinate which leader with an exploding bar of chocolate? A) Adolf Hitler B) Winston Churchill C) Charles de Gaulle ***(1pt)***

2. The roadside sign for a hospital's A&E department has a white H on what colour background? A) Red B) Blue C) Yellow ***(1pt)***

3. Bewitched, Bothered and Bewildered is a song from which musical? A) Pajama Game B) Sweet Charity C) Pal Joey ***(2pts)***

4. In the 2005 film version of 'The Magic Roundabout', Robbie Williams voiced which character? A) Brian B) Dougal C) Zebedee ***(2pts)***

5. Which of these is an obsolete style of shoe? A) Bowler B) Fedora C) Trilby *(3pts)*

6. In the children's TV show 'Rastamouse', who is President of Mouseland? A) Cheddar Gorge B) Red Lester C) Wensley Dale ***(3pts)***

7. What is the name of a young beaver? A) Kit B) Cub C) Kid ***(4pts)***

8. Which of these is the name of a training system for runners, which varies pace and distance? A) Fluffkek B) Flatulek C) Fartlek ***(4pts)***

9. The Zentralfriedhof, Vienna is one of world's largest? A) Zoos B) Cemeteries C) Cafes ***(5pts)***

10. The world leader of the Salvation Army holds what title? A) Captain B) Major C) General

ACCUMULATED INFORMATION

1. In US politics, how many senators represent each state?

In terms of area, which is the largest island in the Mediterranean?

3. Which UK Sunday paper is the oldest, having been launched in 1791?

4. In which novel do the characters Sebastian Flyte and Charles Ryder appear?

5. Which one of Henry VIII's wives was married to him for the longest time?

6. What was traditionally rung in Lloyds of London before announcements to signal that a ship was overdue or lost at sea?

7. Which school did comic character Billy Bunter attend?

8. Whom did Andy Murray defeat 6-4, 7-5, 6-4 in his first Wimbledon Singles Final in 2013?

9. Who is the founder of the Glastonbury Music Festival?

10. The vowels have been removed from which phrase (below) used on occasion by rail companies?

L VSN THLN

GOING UP! ANSWERS

1. B) WINSTON CHURCHILL

2. A) RED

3. C) PAL JOEY

4. D) DOUGAL

5. C) TRILBY

6. C) WENSLEYDALE

7. A) KIT

8. C) FARTLEK

9. B) CEMETERIES

10. C) GENERAL

ACCUMULATED INFORMATION ANSWERS

1. 2
2. SICILY
3. THE OBSERVER
4. BRIDESHEAD REVISITED
5. CATHERINE OF ARAGON
6. THE LUTINE BELL
7. GREYFRIARS
8. NOVAK DJOKOVIC
9. MICHAEL EAVIS
10. LEAVES ON THE LINE

Answer 6

ANAGRAMS

Can you work these ciphers out?

1. FINE IN TORN JEANS *(Actress 8,7)*
2. RASHLY BRED GENT *(MP turned celebrity 5,9)*
3. I AM A RIGHT DEATH CASE *(Titled Crime Writer 4,6,8)*
4. TAKEN IT FOR RIDE *(Jockey 7,7)*
5. BRITTLE STAGNATION *(TV Show 8,3,6)*
6. FEND SIR *(TV sitcom 7)*
7. WIRELESS ANIMAL *(Sports star 6,8)*
8. PARK FARMLAND *(Premier Manager 5,7)*
9. BASIL RIDE *(Actor 5,4)*
10. BLANDER BY THEN *(TV actress 6,7)*
11. JOIN HORN BOSS *(Politician 5,7)*
12. YODEL UNFIT *(TV show 4,2,4)*
13. THRONE RUN MAN *(Football legend Covid-19 victim 6,6)*
14. END OF MINING *(Animated film 7,4)*
15. FILCH THE BONELESS MEAT *(Oscar winning film 3,7,2,3,5)*

....

A COUPLE OF HEAD SCRATCHERS!

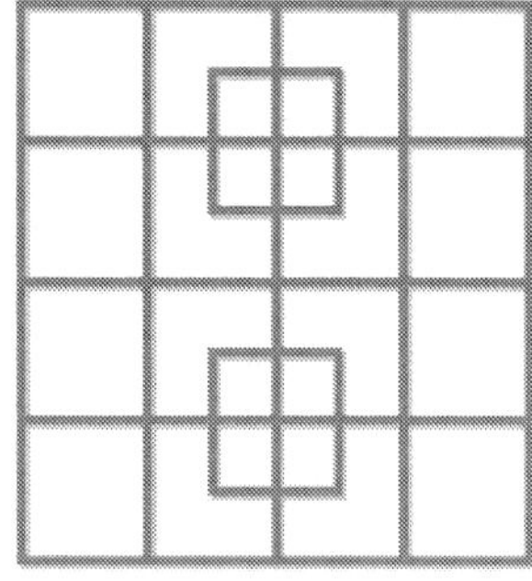

1. How many squares in the picture?

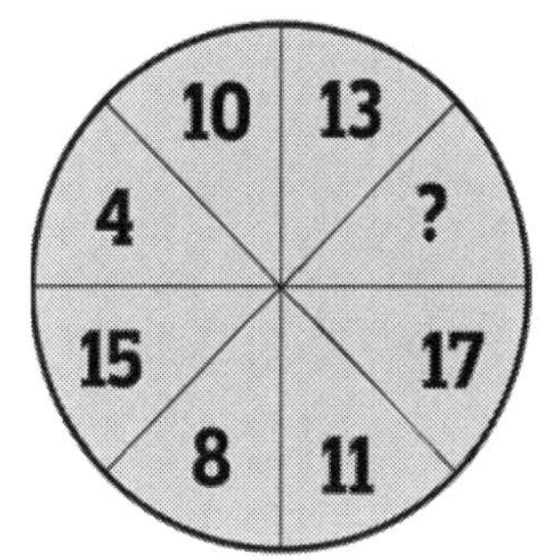

2. What is the missing number?

ANAGRAMS ANSWERS

1. JENNIFER ANISTON

2. GYLES BRANDRETH

3. DAME AGATHA CHRISTIE

4. FRANKIE DETTORI

5. BRITAIN'S GOT TALENT

6. FRIENDS

7. SERENA WILLIAMS

8. FRANK LAMPARD

9. IDRIS ELBA

10. BRENDA BLETHYN

11. BORIS JOHNSON

12. LINE OF DUTY

13. NORMAN HUNTER

14. FINDING NEMO

15. THE SILENCE OF THE LAMBS

A COUPLE OF HEAD SCRATCHERS! ANSWERS

1. 40 SQUARES IN THE PICTURE - Most people get this wrong!

2. THE MISSING NUMBER IS 6 - Opposite numbers add up to 21.

CAPTAIN'S LOG

Name the 10 Captains

RIDDLES

1. Which is faster, hot or cold?
2. Forwards I am heavy, backwards I am not. What am I?
3. What's never used until it is broken?
4. What starts with E and ends in E but only has one letter?
5. When is your uncle's sister not your aunt?

CAPTAIN'S LOG ANSWERS

1. JACK SPARROW *(PIRATES OF CARIBBEAN)*

2. CAPTAIN PUGWASH

3. CAPTAIN MORGAN *(RUM)*

4. CAPTAIN CAVEMAN

5. STEPH HOUGHTON ***(ENGLAND WOMEN'S FOOTBALL)***

6. CAPTAIN ROBERT FALCON SCOTT

7. CAPTAIN EDWARD SMITH *(TITANIC)*

8. HAN SOLO ***(STAR WARS)***

9. KATHRYN JANEWAY *(USS VOYAGER)*

10. MICHAEL CLARKE *(AUSTRALIA CRICKET)*

RIDDLES ANSWERS

1. HOT. YOU CAN EASILY CATCH COLD!
2. TON
3. EGG
4. AN ENVELOPE
5. WHEN SHE'S YOUR MOTHER

EXPAND YOUR MIND

1. A Vietnamese Pot Belly is what type of animal?

2. Which female singer has had hits including *Beating Heart* and *How Long Will I Love You*?

3. Which author's work includes *Rebecca*, *The Birds* and *Jamaica Inn*?

4. Since 2007 which London Station is the terminus for the London, Belgium, France and Netherlands Eurostar service?

5. Which musical movie features the characters Sandy Olsson and Danny Zuko?

6. Who was the pioneering female pilot who became the first woman to fly solo from England to Australia in 1930?

7. Which Jamaican runner is an 11-time world champion and holds the record at 100 & 200 metres?

8. How many major time zones does the world have?

9. Which element is a poisonous gas that combines with sodium to form table salt?

10. Which organs of the human body are affected by the disorder Bright's Disease?

AILMENTS

1. The disease rickets is caused by a deficiency in which vitamin?

2. By what name was COVID-19 more familiarly known?

3. What does the acronym ADHD stand for?

4. Dr Edward Jenner developed the technique of vaccination to combat which disease?

5. Florence Nightingale came to fame as a result of her nursing of soldiers during which war?

6. The MMR vaccine is given to prevent what?

7. Pediculus humanus capitis is the Latin name for which parasite?

8. Which part of the body would be affected, if you suffered from Quinsy?

9. Spread by the bite of an infected Tsetse fly, how is the disease Human African Trypanosomiasis more commonly known?

10. How is the childhood illness pertussismore commonly known?

EXPAND YOUR MIND ANSWERS

1. PIG

2. ELLIE GOULDING

3. DAPHNE DU MAURIER

4. LONDON ST PANCRAS

5. GREASE

6. AMY JOHNSON

7. USAIN BOLT

8. 24

9. CHLORINE

10. KIDNEYS

AILMENTS ANSWERS

1. D

2. CORONAVIRUS

3. ATTENTION DEFICIT HYPERACTIVITY DISORDER

4. SMALLPOX

5. CRIMEAN WAR

6. MEASLES, MUMPS, RUBELLA (GERMAN MEASLES)

7. HEAD LOUSE

8. THROAT OR TONSILS

9. SLEEPING SICKNESS

10. WHOOPING COUGH

DINGBATS

Can you solve these?

1. CUT
THE REST

2. Eye E
Baltic Xept

3. MATE

4. Dazzling
GIBRALTAR

5. Hell 2 Heaven 1

6. 

7. My HOE

8. O ERT O .

9. 

10. 

BRUSH UP YOUR SHAKESPEARE

Who said these lines and in which play by William Shakespeare?

1. Knowing I loved my books, he furnished me from mine own library with volumes that I prize above my dukedom.
2. I'll read enough, when I do see the very book indeed. Where all my sins are writ, and that's myself.
3. Your face, my thane, is a book where men may read strange matters.

DINGBATS ANSWERS

1. A CUT ABOVE THE REST
2. BEFORE THE E AFTER C
3. CHECKMATE
4. BRIGHTON ROCK
5. PARADISE LOST
6. TOUCAN

7. IVANHOE
8. PAINLESS OPERATION
9. BE SEEING YOU
10. ALL ROADS LEAD TO ROME

BRUSH UP YOUR SHAKESPEARE ANSWERS

1. PROSPERO IN THE TEMPEST
2. RICHARD II IN THE PLAY OF THE SAME NAME
3. LADY MACBETH IN MACBETH

ALL KINDS OF EVERYTHING

1. What type of foodstuff is Swiss Chard?

2. In 1995 a British born banker working in Singapore caused mass losses to Barings Bank by fraudulent dealing. Name him.

3. Who is the host of the ITV teatime show, *The Chase*?

4. Where on the outer human body is the thinnest skin?

5. Which former Yorkshire and Middlesex test bowler was appointed as head coach of England cricket in October 2019?

6. Which Stuart monarch was married to Catherine of Braganza?

7. In 2020 who walked 100 lengths of his garden for NHS Charities Together, because our fantastic NHS workers are national heroes, and raised almost £33 million pounds earning himself a knighthood at 100?

8. What is manufactured and named after a village in the Ironbridge Gorge Shropshire?

9. Which Shakespeare play has the characters Prospero and Caliban?

10, If a person is known as a Cantabrigian from which English city would they have originated?

FIRST LINES OF BOOKS

We've rounded up the first lines of some of the world's most famous books. Name them!

1. Far out in the uncharted backwaters of the unfashionable end of the western spiral arm of the Galaxy, lies a small unregarded yellow sun.

2. It was a bright cold day in April, and the clocks were striking thirteen.

3. It is a truth universally acknowledged, that a single man in possession, of a good fortune, must be in want of a wife.

4. All children, except one, grow up.

5. You better not tell nobody but God.

6. "Where's Papa going with that axe?" Said Fern to her mother as they were setting the table for breakfast.

7. There was no possibility of taking a walk that day.

8. It is cold at 6:40 in the morning of a March day in Paris, and seems even colder when a man is about to be executed by firing squad.

9. Mrs. Bantry was dreaming. Her sweet peas had just taken a First at the flower show.

10. Nobody was really surprised when it happened, not really, not at the subconscious level where savage things grow.

ALL KINDS OF EVERYTHING ANSWERS

1. A GREEN LEAFY VEGETABLE *(Like beet)*

2. NICK LEESON

3. BRADLEY WALSH

4. EYELIDS

5. CHRIS SILVERWOOD

6. CHARLES II

7. CAPTAIN SIR TOM MOORE

8. CHINA AND PORCELAIN FIGURES

9. THE TEMPEST

10. CAMBRIDGE

FIRST LINES OF BOOKS ANSWERS

1. HITCHHIKERS GUIDE TO THE GALAXY BY DOUGLAS ADAMS

2. 1984 BY GEORGE ORWELL

3. PRIDE AND PREJUDICE BY JANE AUSTEN

4. PETER PAN BY JM BARRIE

5. THE COLOR PURPLE BY ALICE WALKER

6. CHARLOTTE'S WEB BY EB WHITE

7. JANE EYRE BY CHARLOTTE BRONTE

8. THE DAY OF THE JACKAL BY FREDERICK FORSYTH

9. THE BODY IN THE LIBRARY BY AGATHA CHRISTIE

10. CARRIE BY STEPHEN KING

CARRYING ON

Each answer contains a word that is repeated in the answer to the next question

1. Will Smith plays a rapper who left Philadelphia to live with wealthy relatives. Which sit-com?

2. Who did Flora McDonald help to escape to the Isle of Skye?

3. Who appeared as himself to sing *Behind Closed Doors* in *Every Which Way But Loose* ?

4. Which novel by Irwin Shaw told the story of the Jordache family?

5. In which film is the lead villain called Scaramanga?

6. The building of what was completed in May 1937 in San Francisco?

7. Which film recounted the true story of the 1944 Battle of Arnhelm?

8. Bathsheba Everdene is the heroine of which Thomas Hardy novel?

9. What was The Beatles first ever Number 1 single in the UK?

10. In which 2000 film did Jim Carrey play a character suffering from schizophrenia?

ROBIN AND THE MERRY MEN

1. What kind of animal did Disney use to portray Robin Hood in their animated version of the story?

2. Which right-hand man of Robin Hood is renowned for his size and strength?

3. When Kevin Costner played Robin Hood on film, who played Maid Marian?

4. What is the name of the tyrannical prince, a sworn enemy of Robin Hood?

5. In which English county is Sherwood Forest, the hideout of Robin Hood?

6. Which man of the cloth did Robin Hood reputedly fight at Fountain Dale before inviting him to join the band of outlaws?

7. What is the name of Robin Hood's minstrel?

8. The 2018 version of *Robin Hood* is a quasi-contemporary retelling of the Robin Hood legend, and follows his training by John to steal from the Sheriff of Nottingham. Who played Robin?

9. Who starred in the 1950s TV series *The Adventures of Robin Hood*?

10. Who played the title role in the 1938 film *The Adventures of Robin Hood*?

CARRYING ON ANSWERS

1. THE PRINCE OF BELAIR

2. BONNIE PRINCE CHARLIE

3. CHARLIE RICH

4. RICH MAN, POOR MAN

5. THE MAN WITH THE GOLDEN GUN

6. THE GOLDEN GATE BRIDGE

7. A BRIDGE TOO FAR

8. FAR FROM THE MADDING CROWD

9. FROM ME TO YOU

10. ME, MYSELF AND IRENE

ROBIN AND THE MERRY MEN ANSWERS

1. A FOX
2. LITTLE JOHN
3. MARY ELIZABETH MASTRANTONIO
4. PRINCE JOHN
5. NOTTINGHAMSHIRE
6. FRIAR TUCK
7. ALLAN-A-DALE
8. TARON EGERTON
9. RICHARD GREENE
10. ERROL FLYNN

Question 2

A WIDTH OF WISDOM

1. Who was appointed UK Secretary of State for Education in July 2019?
2. In the UK we call them waistcoats, but what are they known as in the US?
3. In the film The Jungle Book, what type of creature is Bagheera?
4. Name the oldest commercial airline still operating with its original name?
5. Said to have originated in the City of Bath. What is a 'Sally Lunn'?
6. A rhinoceros' horn is made from what?
7. Who was the first British astronaut in space?
8. What is the largest brass instrument in an orchestra?
9. By what name is the blackthorn bush known?
10. Which is the largest lake by size in the UK?

LOOK OUT FOR MORE BOOKS BY CHRIS SMART AND MIKE LEWIS

BLOCKBUSTERS (1)

1. What **S** is the inky secretion of Cuttlefish?
2. What does **ABV** stand for on a bottle of beer?
3. Which **HGOB** was one of the 7 wonders of the world whose definite location is unknown?
4. Which **I L M H I S F** is a song synonymous with Tony Bennett?
5. What **L** is a type of Sea snail or an underwater explosive mine attached to the hull of ships?
6. What **AM** was the convict in the novel *Great Expectations* who was befriended by Pip?
7. What **TVRD** is trophy awarded to the ladies Wimbledon singles champion?
8. What **NMGTT**. is said to be the hymn played by the band as the Titanic was sinking?
9. What **M** is an African country whose capital is Maputo?
10. Which **LJB** had hit songs titled *Let The Heartaches Begin* and *It Ain't Easy?*

A huge Inquizitors show at Celtic Manor Resort

A WIDTH OF WISDOM ANSWERS

1. GAVIN WILLIAMSON

2. VESTS

3. BLACK PANTHER

4. KLM

5. A BUN *(PART BUN, PART BREAD, PART CAKE)*

6. KERATIN *(THE SAME TYPE OF PROTEIN THAT MAKES UP HAIR AND FINGERNAILS)*

7. HELEN SHARMAN

8. TUBA

9. SLOE

10. LOUGH NEAGH

BLOCKBUSTERS (1) ANSWERS

1. SEPIA

2. ALCOHOL BY VOLUME

3. THE HANGING GARDENS OF BABYLON

4. I LEFT MY HEART IN SAN FRANCISCO

5. LIMPET

6. ABEL MAGWITCH

7. THE VENUS ROSEWATER DISH

8. NEARER MY GOD TO THEE

9. MOZAMBIQUE

10. LONG JOHN BALDRY

CHINESE GETAWAY

1. The Renminbi is official currency - by what name is it more commonly known?

2. On a Chinese Takeaway menu what are Wontons?

3. 6,000 life-sized sculptures were unearthed in 1974 by Chinese farmers digging a well - how are they known?

4. Because of its shape what name was given to the Beijing National Stadium at the 2008 Olympic Games?

5. In the 1970s TV series Kung Fu, who played the wandering Shaolin monk called Caine?

6. What is the standard most spoken Chinese language?

7. China Girl is the title of a 1983 No 2 hit for which singer?

8. Which one of these is the Chinese Year for 2020? a. DRAGON b. RAT c. ROOSTER.

9. What shape is the playing board in the game Chinese Chequers?

10. Which scented large flowering plant is the national flower of China?

OH MATRON!

1. In which horror spoof *Carry On* film did Kenneth Williams play a character inspired by Frankenstein?

2. In which year was the last *Carry On* film released?

3. Which South African actor, known as 'the grand old man of dirty laughter', star of 19 *Carry On* films, died on stage in 1976 aged 62?

4. What was the title of the TV series in which the characters and comedy style of the *Carry On* film series were adapted ?

5. Which American entertainer replaced Sid James in the 1967 *Carry On...Follow That Camel* ?

6. Who played the title role in the 1992 *Carry On Columbus* ?

7. In 1964, what was the first *Carry On* film to feature Barbara Windsor?

8. Who played the Khasi of Kalabar in *Carry On Up The Khyber* ?

9. Who directed the majority of the *Carry On* films?

10. Which *Carry On* film featured the characters Captain Fancy, Sergeant Jock Strapp, Reverend Flasher and Madame Desiree?

CHINESE GETAWAY ANSWERS

1. YUAN

2. DUMPLINGS

3. TERRA COTTA ARMY

4. BIRDSNEST

5. DAVID CARRADINE

6. MANDARIN

7. DAVID BOWIE

8. B) RAT

9. STAR SHAPE

10. PEONY

OH MATRON! ANSWERS

1. CARRY ON SCREAMING?

2. 1992 *(Carry on Columbus, 31st and final release)*

3. SID JAMES

4. CARRY ON LAUGHING

5. PHIL SILVERS

6. JIM DALE

7. CARRY ON SPYING

8. KENNETH WILLIAMS

9. GERALD THOMAS

10. CARRY ON DICK

WORKS OF ART

10 famous paintings. Can you identify the painters?

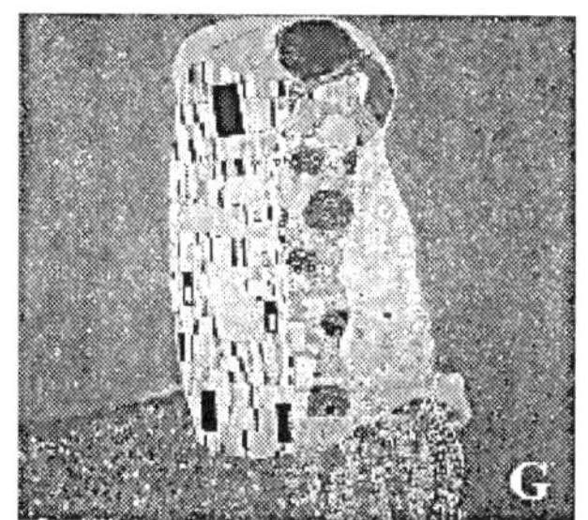

FOUR-LETTER WORDS

All answers are 4 letter words - beginning with F

1. First name of the man who had a hit with Blueberry Hill.
2. Surname of the Labour Party leader from 1980 -1983.
3. North American broad bean.
4. Region north of the Firth of Forth
5. Roman public meeting places.

WORKS OF ART ANSWERS

A. Whistler's Mother - JAMES ABBOTT McNEILL WHISTLER

B. Campbell's Soup Can - ANDY WARHOL

C. Stratford Mill - JOHN CONSTABLE

D. Mona Lisa - LEONARDO DA VINCI

E. Starry Night - VINCENT VAN GOGH

F. The Son of Man - RENE MAGRITTE

G. The Kiss - GUSTAV KLIMT

H. The Scream - EDVARD MUNCH

I. Self Portrait - PABLO PICASSO

J. The Night Watch - REMBRANDT HARMENSZOON VAN RIJN

FOUR-LETTER WORDS ANSWERS

1. FATS (DOMINO)

2. (MICHAEL) FOOT
3. FAVA
4. FIFE
5. FORA

DOCTOR, DOCTOR

1. Which doctor, turned author wrote Jurassic Park and The Andromeda Strain?
2. Dr Hastings Banda was president, prime minister and dictator of which African country for 30 years?
3. What was the first name of paediatrician Dr Spock?
4. Name the BBC One drama television series that was first broadcast on 9 September 2015 and starred Suranne Jones.
5. Who might use a nebuliser?
6. Warfarin, once used a rat poison, is used to treat what medical conditions?
7. What is the ancient practice of sticking needles into a patient called?
8. Which BAFTA award winning comedian and presenter is still a registered GP?
9. Which is the longest bone in the body?
10. Name the American medical drama that starred English actor Hugh Lawrie and ran for 177 episodes.

WORDS AND NUMBERS (1)

30 point round

1. Every Australian citizen is entitled to a portrait of whom to hang in their home?
A) The Queen B) Crocodile Dundee C) Dame Edna Everage (1pt)

2. Which of these is not a station on a London Monopoly board?
A) Marleybone B) Kings Cross C) Waterloo (1pt)

3. At what distance did Dina Asher-Smith win Gold at the 2019 World Championships?
A) 100 metres B) 200 metres C) 100 metres hurdles (2 pts)

4. In TV's Downton Abbey, who is the butler? A) Mr Carson B) Mr Mason C) Mr Bates (2pts)

5. £sd came to an end. Which year was the UK decimalised? A) 1970 B)1971 C)1972 (3pts)

6. Originally associated with Berwick-upon-Tweed, what are Berwick Cockles?
A) Seafood B) Sweetbreads C) Mint Sweets (3pts)

7. Car tyres inflated to 2BAR pressure, the approximate equivalent in PSI is? A) 27 B) 29 C) 31 (4pts)

8. Where does a pelagic bird feed? A) In the air A) Out at sea B) On the ground (4pts)

9. Donald Trump is the 45th President. Who was the 38th? A) G Ford B) R Nixon C) J Carter (5pts)

10. In 1997 the Cassini Huygens Space probe orbited a planet? A) Mars B) Saturn C) Jupiter (5pts)

DOCTOR, DOCTOR ANSWERS

1. MICHAEL CRICHTON

2. MALAWI

3. BENJAMIN

4. DOCTOR FOSTER

5. SOMEONE WITH ASTHMA

6. STROKES AND THROMBOSIS *(ANTI COAGULANT)*

7. ACUPUNCTURE

8. HARRY HILL

9. FEMUR *(THIGH BONE))*

10. HOUSE

WORDS AND NUMBERS (1) ANSWERS

1. A) THE QUEEN - *1 point*

2. C) WATERLOO - *1 point*

3. B) 200 METRES - *2 points*

4. A) MR CARSON - *2 points*

5. B) 1971 - *3 points*

6. C) MINT SWEETS - *3 points*

7. B) 29 - *4 points*

8. B) OUT AT SEA - *4 points*

9. A) GERALD FORD - *5 points*

10. B) SATURN - *5 points*

Question 6

NAME THAT YEAR

Can you name the year that these songs reached number one in the UK?

1. *Fireflies* by Owl City *(3 weeks at top)*

2. *Heart* by The Pet Shop Boys *(3 weeks at top)*

3. *Long Live Love* by Sandie Shaw (*3 weeks at top)*

4. *Whiter Shade Of Pale* by Procol Harum (*6 weeks at top)*

5. *Where Is The Love* by The Black Eyed Peas (*6 weeks at top)*

6. *She* by Charles Aznavour *(4 weeks at top)*

7. *I Believe I Can Fly* by R. Kelly *(3 weeks at top)*

8. *Rollercoaster* by B*witched *(2 weeks at top)*

9. *Return To Sender* by Elvis Presley *(3 weeks at top)*

10. *Frankie* by Sister Sledge *(4 weeks at top)*

COMMON SENSE

1. In which British city will you find Waverley station?

2. The Swiss Re Tower, 30 St Mary Axe was added to the London skyline in 2004. By what name is it more familiarly known?

3. In which British city will you find the Bridgewater Concert Hall?

4. Which actor, who died in January 2014, was best known for playing Trigger and Owen Newitt?

5. What kind of vegetable is 'devil's apron'?

6. In which year did George W Bush become US president; USS Cole is bombed in Aden; the *I Love You* virus affects computers world-wide?

7. What unusual weapon was used to kill Leon Trotsky in 1940?

8. What does ABTA stand for?

9. Leicester City now play at the King Power Stadium (formerly known as Walkers Stadium). Where was their previous home ground?

10. At which racecourse is the Welsh Grand National held?

NAME THAT YEAR ANSWERS

1. 2010
2. 1988
3. 1965
4. 1967
5. 2003
6. 1974

7. 1997
8. 1998
9. 1962
10. 1985

COMMON SENSE ANSWERS

1. EDINBURGH
2. THE GHERKIN
3. MANCHESTER
4. ROGER LLOYD-PACK *(Only Fools & Horses and The Vicar of Dibley)*
5. SEAWEED (KELP)

6. 2000
7. AN ICE PICK
8. ASSOCIATION OF BRITISH TRAVEL AGENTS
9. FILBERT STREET
10. CHEPSTOW

LANDMARKS AROUND THE WORLD

Can you name them?

WHO'S THE DOCTOR?

13 actors have played the title role in Dr Who on BBC TV.
Can you name them?

LANDMARKS AROUND THE WORLD ANSWERS

1. ARC DE TRIOMPHE, PARIS

2. BERKELEY CASTLE, GLOUCESTERSHIRE

3. ACROPOLIS, ATHENS

4. NIAGARA FALLS, NEW YORK STATE

5. POMPEII, NEAR NAPLES

6. BLACKPOOL TOWER, LANCASHIRE

7. AUSCHWITZ, OŚWIĘCIM

8. TAJ MAHAL, AGRA

9. HADRIAN'S WALL, NORTH OF ENGLAND

10. MOUNT KILIMANJARO, TANZANIA

WHO'S THE DOCTOR? ANSWERS

1. WILLIAM HARTNELL
2. PATRICK TROUGHTON
3. JON PERTWEE
4. TOM BAKER
5. PETER DAVISON
6. COLIN BAKER
7. SYLVESTER McCOY
8. PAUL McGANN
9. CHRISTOPHER ECCLESTON
10. DAVID TENNANT
11. MATT SMITH
12. PETER CAPALDI
13. JODIE WHITTAKER

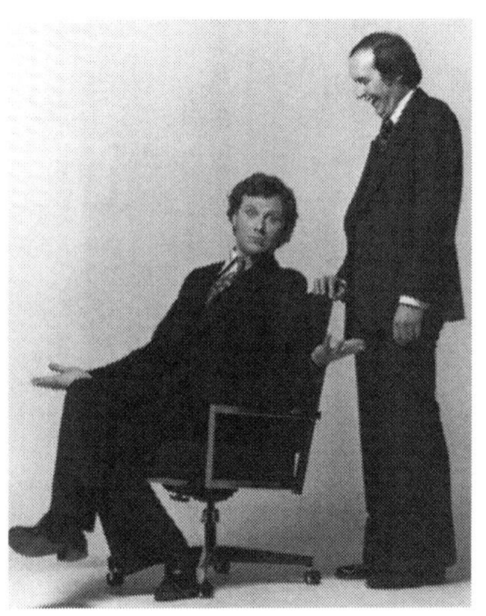

Co-author Mike with the 6th Doctor Colin Baker back in 1986

CONNECTIONS (3)

Answer the 10 questions and for a bonus find a connection

1. Which Oscar-winning 2009 Kathryn Bigelow film features a three-man US Army Explosive Ordnance Disposal team during the Iraq War?

2. In geology, how is a planar fracture or discontinuity in a volume of rock, across which there has been significant displacement, better known?

3. Which Elvis Presley song, based on the tune of a Civil War ballad, was released in 1956, 2 months before the movie of the same name?

4. What title did Baroness Marie Christine Agnes Hedwig Ida von Reibnitz adopt when she married into British Royalty in 1978?

5. In the hit US TV comedy series *Sex and the City*, how is John James Preston, Carrie's on/off boyfriend / husband, better known?

6. Dactyloscopy is the technical term for the identification of what?

7. Which 1978 film featuring Clint Eastwood as prize-fighting trucker Philo Beddoe, had a theme song performed by Eddie Rabbitt?

8. Name the metropolitan county in the North East region of England around the mouths of 2 rivers. It came into existence in 1974.
9. What structure was bought in 1968 by entrepreneur Robert McCulloch, allegedly by mistake, and now stands at Lake Havasu City in Arizona?

10. What was the name of the 1987 hit single by footballers Glenn Hoddle and Chris Waddle, which reached No12 in the UK charts?

Now name the connection!

A MOTLEY COLLECTION

1. Which comedy actress and writer played the characters Mrs Merton and Denise Royle?
2. The United Arab Emirates is a federation of how many Emirates?
3. What is the term for a baby Koala?
4. Which 'All Saint' did Liam Gallager divorce in 2014?
5. In which city would you find the i360 tower?
6. Which Conservative MP became 'Leader of the House' in July 2019?
7. 'The Chronicles of Narnia' is a children's book series written by which author?
8. 'Food Glorious Food' is a song from which British musical?
9. Which epic fantasy novel is set on the fictional continents of Westeros and Essos?
10. If one side of a square is ten centimetres long, what is the circumference?

CONNECTIONS (3) ANSWERS

1. THE HURT **LOCKER**

2. **FAULT** LINE

3. LOVE ME **TENDER**

4. PRINCESS **MICHAEL** OF KENT

5. (MR) **BIG**

6. FINGER**PRINTS**

7. EVERY WHICH WAY BUT **LOOSE**

8. TYNE AND **WEAR**

9. LONDON **BRIDGE**

10. DIAMOND **LIGHTS**

Connection: WORDS USED WITH FOOT

A MOTLEY COLLECTION ANSWERS

1. CAROLINE AHERNE

2. 7

3. JOEY

4. NICOLE APPLETON

5. BRIGHTON

6. JACOB REES-MOGG

7. CS LEWIS

8. OLIVER

9. GAME OF THRONES (A SONG OF FIRE AND ICE)

10. 40cm

THE EYES HAVE IT

1. What eye condition is also the name of a waterfall?

2. Which species of creature has the largest eyes?

3. You can lose a contact lens behind your eyeball. True or False.

4. *Eye Level*, the theme from TV Van Der Valk, reached number one in 1972. Who had the hit?

5. What road safety aid was invented by Percy Shaw 1934?

6. Which actresses eyes did Kim Carnes sing about in a 1981 hit?

7. What is the title of the film in which Helen Mirren plays Colonel Katherine Powell, a UK-based military officer, in command of a top secret drone operation to capture terrorists in Kenya?

8. What connects the singer Gabrielle, Admiral Lord Nelson and Rooster Cogburn in *True Grit*?

9. In the *Oklahoma* song *Oh What A Beautiful Mornin'* what creature's eye is said to be as high as the corn?

10. Wearing glasses all the time weakens your eyes.True or False?

AND THE WINNER IS....

1. Who was the first actor to win a posthumous best actor Oscar?

2. Who was the first person to win a Grammy, an Oscar, a Tony and have a number one hit in the UK and the US?

3. Which woman, by height, is the littlest woman in the 2019 movie *Little Women*; Florence Pugh, Emma Watson or Saoirse Ronan?

4. Given normal traffic, how far could you legally travel on a British motorway in the time to watch *The Irishman* (2019) in full?

5. Which Korean film surprisingly won the Academy Award for Best 2019 Picture?

6. Joaquin Phoenix won best actor award at the 2020 Oscar ceremony. In which film did he star?

7. Which actor has an Oscar for producing *12 Years a Slave* but despite several acting nominations, has yet to win one for performing?

8. Which 3 films have won 11 Academy Awards?

9. What classic 1934 movie was the first film to sweep the five major categories— Best Picture, Director, Actor, Actress, and Screenplay?

10. The youngest ever Oscar winner was just 10 years old - for Best Supporting Actress in 1973. Who is she?

THE EYES HAVE IT ANSWERS

1. CATARACT

2. THE GIANT SQUID *(can be 500mm across)*

3. FALSE *(enclosed in a pouch, conjunctival sac)*

4. SIMON PARK ORCHESTRA

5. CAT'S EYES

6. BETTE DAVIS

7. EYE IN THE SKY

8. ALL WORE EYEPATCHES

9. ELEPHANT

10. FALSE

AND THE WINNER IS... AWARDS ANSWERS

1. PETER FINCH *(For Network in 1976)*

2. BARBRA STREISAND

3. FLORENCE PUGH *(Pugh 1.62, Watson 1.65, Ronan 1.68)*

4. 245 MILES *(3hrs 30mins long)*

5. PARASITE

6. JOKER

7. BRAD PITT

8. BEN HUR, TITANIC, LORD OF THE RINGS:RETURN OF THE KING

9. IT HAPPENED ONE NIGHT

10. TATUM O'NEAL *(for Paper Moon)*

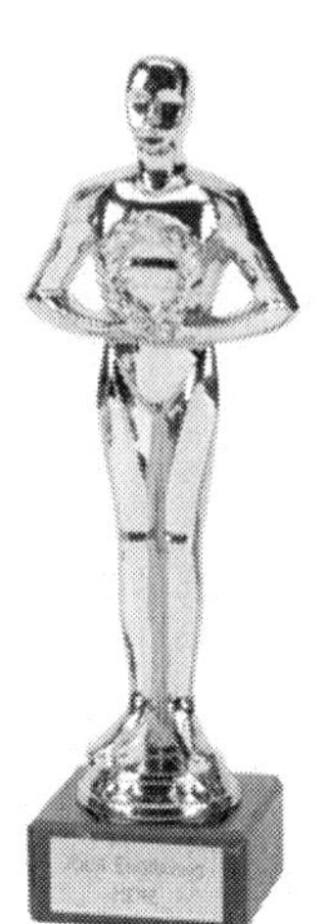

1066 AND ALL THAT

1. Upon which hill was the Battle of Hastings fought?
2. On what date was the Battle fought, and how long did it last?
3. What links a battle fought earlier in 1066 and a Premiership football stadium?
4. Which famous piece of needlework is a major source of information about events around 1066?
5. An investigation by Channel 4's Time Team concluded the battle – and the death of England's last Anglo-Saxon king – was actually centred on a fourth site. What modern traffic site did they suggest?
6. However the official historical version states that Harold fell where today's English Heritage visitors can stand. Where?
7. How does the shape of a Norman shield remind one of flying?
8. In which historical building was William the Conqueror, crowned King of England?
9. What was the most feared weapon wielded by the Saxon soldiers?
10. Why were many Norman soldiers able to look down on the English opponents they were fighting?

FOLLOW ON (2)

The last letter of answer 1 is the first letter on answer 2 and so on

1. Into which sea does the east side of the Germany's Kiel Canal flow?
2. Which element has Atomic No 17 and is second lightest of the halogens?
3. Which area in London gives its name to film comedies made there between 1947 and 1957?
4. What is the birthstone for the month of January?
5. By what name is one of many types of Chinese transnational organized crime syndicates known?
6. What is the surname of Wendy, John and Michael in the Peter Pan stories?
7. Which fabled creature has the body and legs of a lion and the wings and head of an eagle?
8. 8th August 1945. Upon which Japanese city did an atom bomb fall?
9. Name the only survivor of the ship, the Pequod, who narrated the tale of *Moby Dick*?
10. What name is used to describe an act of seizing land in an opportunistic or unlawful manner?

1066 AND ALL THAT ANSWERS

1. SENLAC HILL

2. A) 14 OCTOBER 1066 B) ABOUT 9 HOURS

3. STAMFORD BRIDGE

4. BAYEUX TAPESTRY

5. A MINI ROUNDABOUT ON THE A2100 JUST OUTSIDE BATTLE

6. SITE OF HIGH ALTAR IN BATTLE ABBEY

7. IT WAS KITE SHAPED

8. WESTMINSTER ABBEY

9. A BATTLE AXE *(Held in both hands)*

10. THEY FOUGHT ON HORSEBACK *WHILST THE ENGLISH FOUGHT ON FOOT*

FOLLOW ON (2) ANSWERS

1. BALTIC

2. CHLORINE

3. EALING

4. GARNET

5. TRIAD

6. DARLING

7. GRIFFIN

8. NAGASAKI

9. ISHMAEL

10. LANDGRAB

A ROUND OF DRINKS

1. Who wrote Drink Up Thy Zider, originally a small hit in 1966 and then inherited by Bristol C as their entrance music?
2. What which fruit is the drink Perry distilled?
3. What brand of beer was advertised on TV in no-nonsense style by comedy star Peter Kay?
4. Along which river and its tributaries do the German vineyards lie?
5. Which wine has the varieties Malmsey and Sercial?
6. What three letter word is Chinese for tea?
7. Who wrote the poem The Rime of the Ancient Mariner which contains the line, "Water, water everywhere, not any drop to drink"?
8. Who wanted to 'go home' after too much Coor's beer?
9. Which Scottish River supplies over 90% of the water used in Whisky manufacture?
10. From what country does Tequila originate?

BLOCKBUSTERS (2)

1. What **I** are lines on a weather map of atmospheric pressure?
2. In the Old Testament book of Judges what **TJOAA** did Samson use to kill 1000 Philistines?
3. What **S** can be a dark green winter vegetable and a hotel in London?
4. What **LM** is the actor who played Major Reisman in the film *The Dirty Dozen* ?
5. What **WC** is the common everyday name for the medical condition Scriveners palsy?
6. What **OTSWYL** is a famous song from the musical *My Fair Lady* ?
7. Hans Solo's space craft in Star Wars was named The **MF**
8. What S is the seaside resort where the first Butlins opened in 1936?
9. What **L** is the main ingredient of the Dish, Dublin Lawyer?
10. What **PD** was the byname used by former president of Haiti, Francois Duvalier?

A ROUND OF DRINKS ANSWERS

1. ADGE CUTLER

2. PEARS

3. JOHN SMITH'S

4. THE RHINE

5. MADEIRA

6. CHA

7. SAMUEL TAYLOR COLERIDGE

8. E.T.

9. RIVER SPEY

10. MEXICO

Answer 1

BLOCKBUSTERS (2) ANSWERS

1. ISOBARS

2. THE JAWBONE OF AN ASS

3. SAVOY

4. LEE MARVIN

5. WRITERS CRAMP

6. ON THE STREET WHERE YOU LIVE

7. MILLENNIUM FALCON

8. SKEGNESS

9. LOBSTER

10. PAPA DOC

Answer 8

THREE WORDS

Every answer contains 3 words

1. In The TV show *To The Manor Born*, what character is played by Penelope Keith?
2. Which Anglo-Saxon King ruled England from 1042 to 1066?
3. Published in 1852 which anti-slavery novel was written by Harriet Beecher Stowe?
4. Which football club's home ground is at The Hawthorns?
5. In the DIY world what does MDF stand for?
6. In 1969 who became the first person to sail single-handed non-stop around the world?
7. What are Prince Harry's three middle names?
8. In the photo camera world what does SLR stand for?
9. Who is credited with inventing the first TV set?
10. Who assassinated Martin Luther King in 1968?

EXTENDED ROUND (2)
GIRLS ALOUD

An extended round is great to add variety to a quiz night. Sheets are handed out at the beginning of the quiz and answers then have to be completed at a later stage of the quiz - quite often the half-time break. Often this takes the form of a Picture Round. However there are other options. This round is a simple job of listing as many nominated hits as you can within a specified time. See the instruction below. The complete list of possible answers is shown on the following page. Good luck.

Name as many of the Top 10 Hits of
***GIRLS ALOUD** as you can in 10 minutes!*

THREE WORDS ANSWERS

1. AUDREY FFORBES HAMILTON

2. EDWARD THE CONFESSOR

3. UNCLE TOMS CABIN

4. WEST BROMWICH ALBION

5. MEDIUM DENSITY FIBREBOARD

6. ROBIN KNOX JOHNSTON.

7. CHARLES ALBERT DAVID

8. SINGLE LENS REFLEX

9. JOHN LOGIE BAIRD.

10. JAMES EARL RAY

Answer 3

EXTENDED ROUND (2) ANSWERS
GIRLS ALOUD

BIOLOGY
CALL THE SHOTS
CAN'T SPEAK FRENCH
JUMP
I THINK WE'RE ALONE NOW
I'LL STAND BY YOU
LIFE GOT COLD
LONG HOT SUMMER
LOVE MACHINE
THE LOVING KIND
NO GOOD ADVICE
THE PROMISE
SEE THE DAY
SEXY NO NO NO
THE SHOW
SOMETHING KINDA OOOOH
SOUND OF THE UNDERGROUND
UNTOUCHABLE
WAKE ME UP
WHOLE LOTTA HISTORY

SPORTS QUEST

1. What are 28" (71cm) high and 9" (22cm) wide?

2. What was the only Olympic Games to feature the killing of animals, and what was the event?

3. Why did the US boycott the 1980 Olympic Games?

4. Under what name did Robert Craig perform motorcycle stunts?

5. The song Sweet Georgia Brown is the theme song for which popular sporting team?

6. What is the connection between Joe Frazier, Brian Clough, Graham Hill and Chris Broad?

7. In which sport and pastime would a Silver Wilkinson be used?

8. In which sport do competitors change lanes after every lap?

9. Which German legend is the only person to lift the World Cupo as a team captain and manager?

10. What old-fashioned item of clothing is associated with New York's basketball team

A VARIETY OF TRIVIA

1. The Indian city formerly known as Bombay was renamed in 1995. What is its current name?

2. **HE'S LIKE A LAMP I SWEAR** is an anagram of which famous person's name?

3. What type of fruit is a cantaloupe?

4. True or false, The Bahamas is made up of over 700 islands?

5. In which country was the 2019 Women's Football World Cup held?

6. Which grandson of William the Conk was King of England from 1135 to 1154?

7. Who played the part of Hermione Granger in the Harry Potter series of films?

8. What type of creatures are a) Buff Orpingtons and b) Plymouth Rocks?

9. *Lucky*, *Lady Boss* and *Hollywood Wives* are novels by which author?

10. WL Judson invented which useful object in 1891? a) The zip b) The pencil c) The radiator

SPORTS QUEST ANSWERS

1. A SET OF CRICKET STUMPS

2. 1904 OLYMPICS HAD LIVE PIGEON SHOOTING

3. PROTEST ABOUT RUSSIA INVASION OF AFGHANISTAN

4. EVEL KNIEVEL

5. THE HARLEM GLOBETROTTERS

6. ALL HAD SONS WHO FOLLOWED THEM INTO THE SPORT THAT MADE THEM FAMOUS

7. ANGLING *(a type of fly used in Salmon Fishing)*

8. SPEED SKATING

9. FRANZ BECKENBAUER

10. KNICKERBOCKERS *(Sometimes shortened to NY Knicks*

Answer 4

A VARIETY OF TRIVIA ANSWERS

1. MUMBAI.

2. WILLIAM SHAKESPEARE

3. MELON

4. TRUE

5. FRANCE

6. STEPHEN

7. EMMA WATSON

8. CHICKENS

9. JACKIE COLLINS

10. A) THE ZIP

Answer 8

DINOSAUR DILEMMAS

1. How did Sir Richard Owen make an important contribution to the study of dinosaurs?

2. Which dinosaur had a large club tail?

3. On which continent have most dinosaur fossils been found?

4. True or False? Whilst some dinosaurs were as tall as a modern house, some dinosaurs were small enough to have been held in your hand?

5. Stegosaurus was a plant eater but it could look after itself. How did it do that?

6. If Tyrannosaurus Rex was chasing you across a field, how could you outrun it?

7. Early dinosaurs were around at the same time as:

A)Early humans B) Sabre toothed tigers C) Woolly mammoths D) None of this list

8. Brachiosaurus was a tall dinosaur and ate from the treetops. How tall was this long necked dinosaur? A) 3 mtres B) 6 m C) 12m D) 152m

9. What is the name for fossilized Dinosaur droppings
A) Doodicus B) Steptococcus C) Coprolite D) Giganto stink

10. How is the Brontosaurus also known?

OSCAR SONGS

Name the movies that featured these Oscar winning songs

1. 'I'm Gonna Love Me Again'

2. 'Writing's On The Wall'

3. 'Let It Go'

4. 'If I Didn't Have You'

5. 'My Heart Will Go On'

6. 'A Whole New World'

7. 'Take My Breath Away'

8. 'I Just Called To Say I Love You'

9. 'Up Where We Belong'

10. 'Chim Chim Cher-ee

DINOSAUR DILEMMAS ANSWERS

1, HE COINED THE TERM 'DINOSAUR' WHICH MEANS TERRIBLE LIZARD

2. ANKYLOSAURUS

3. NORTH AMERICA

4. TRUE

5. BY SWINGING ITS SPIKY TAIL

6. BY USING A MOTORISED SCOOTER OR SIMILAR

7. NONE OF THE LIST

8. C) 12 METRES (2 Giraffes)

9. C) COPROLITE

10. DIPLODOCUS

OSCAR SONGS ANSWERS

1. ROCKETMAN
2. SPECTRE
3. FROZEN
4. MONSTERS, INC
5. TITANIC
6. ALADDIN
7. TOP GUN
8. THE WOMAN IN RED
9. AN OFFICER AND A GENTLEMAN
10. MARY POPPINS

Answer 5

POP POSERS

1. Who was sitting in the back seat hugging and kissing seven little girls?

2. Which Irish family band, formed in 1970, took their name from Gaelic meaning 'Family'?

3. Which actor duetted with Barbra Streisand on the song *Till I Loved You*, from the never staged musical *Goya: A Life in Song* in 1988?

4. Who was the first of The Beatles to become a grandfather?

5. Which 1979 number one contains the opening line, 'We don't need no education, we don't need no thought control'?

6. Which Australian band had the worldwide smash hit *Down Under*? It reached number 1 in the UK in 1983, their only top 20 success here.

7. What connects the drummer of Queen and the drummer with Duran Duran?

8. Which song was a hit for Buddy Holly, England Sisters, Showaddywaddy and Nick Berry?

9. Which Scottish guitarist, renowned for his work on seminal UK rock 7 roll records Vince Taylor's *Brand New Cadillac* and Johnny Kidd & the Pirates' *Shakin' All Over* died in 2012 aged 73?

10. Which other renowned guitarist (and lead singer) wrote the Tina Turner hit *Private Dancer* and commented that Jeff Beck's guitar solo in her version was the second worst guitar solo in history?

IT'S ALL GREEK!

1. What was the monetary unit of Greece before it converted to the Euro?

2. By what name is the traditional dip or Meze dish whose ingredients include fish roe, lemon juice and olive oil?

3. Which 3rd century BC Macedonian king conquered Persia in 334BC? He died aged just 32.

4. Who composed the musical score for the film *Chariots of Fire*?

5. Who was the goddess of fertility, love and beauty?

6. By what name is Greek based white or rose wine flavoured with pine resin known?

7. Mark Philippoussis, born of Greek descent, represented Australia at which sport?

8. Which TV star created the Greek kebab shop owner Stavros on *Saturday Night Live*?

9. What part of a river will you find in the Greek alphabet?

10. Which of the following is the most visited Greek tourist attraction?
A) ANCIENT SITE OF DELPHI B) ACROPOLIS C) ISLAND OF RHODES

POP POSERS ANSWERS

1. FRED
2. CLANNAD
3. DON JOHNSON
4. RINGO STARR
5. ANOTHER BRICK IN THE WALL BY PINK FLOYD
6. MEN AT WORK
7. BOTH ARE NAMED ROGER TAYLOR
8. HEARTBEAT
9. JOE MORETTI
10. MARK KNOPFLER

Answer 9

IT'S ALL GREEK ANSWERS

1. DRACHMA
2. TARAMASALATA
3. ALEXANDER THE GREAT
4. VANGELIS
5. APHRODITE
6. RETSINA
7. TENNIS
8. HARRY ENFIELD
9. DELTA.
10. C. ISLAND OF RHODES

Answer 8

FIND THE LINK (1)

Answer the questions and find a link

1. What name is given to unsolicited or undesired electronic messages?

2. Who is the former *Question of Sport* captain who won the World Snooker Championship in 1991?

3. Fleetwood Mac have had a string of hit singles in the UK. Which hit was an instrumental and their only number one?

4. What was the occupation of the brothers in the 1954 film *Seven Brides for Seven Brothers*?

5. Which Philadelphia icon bears the inscription "Proclaim Liberty Throughout All the Land Unto All the Inhabitants thereof"?

6. Which English actor is known for his sonorous voice and hearty, king-size portrayals. He was in *Z Cars* between 1962 and 1965?

7. According to the saying, "The devil makes work for ....?

8. What was founded by Ferdinand II of Aragon and Isabella I of Castile to Keep Catholic orthodoxy as the major religion of their kingdom?

9. What is the name of the omnivorous freshwater fish that inhabit South American rivers that are known for their sharp teeth and powerful jaws?

10. Who was the first woman to be nominated for the Vice Presidency of the United States in 2008?

PLANE CRAZY

1. Cary Grant was chased by a crop spraying plane in which 1959 Alfred Hitchcock film?
2. The last line of which classic 1933 film was: 'It wasn't the planes. It was beauty that killed the beast'?
3. In 2020 Squadron Leader Martin Pert will be the leader of which famous top aerobatics team for his third year as Red 1?
4. Name the little girl on the plane who needs a heart transplant in the movie *Airplane* ?
5. What kind of 'hastily' made sleek plane crashed at the Paris Air Show on the 3rd of June 1973?
6. The many planes used for the shooting of which film in the late 1960s were called "the 35th largest air force in the world"?
7. In 1942 Bomber Command formed a special squadron 617 of Lancaster bombers, to be commanded by Wing Commander Guy Gibson for Operation Chastise. What epic film recreated the true story?
8. Which sleek airliner, in service from 1976-2003, had a name that meant harmony'?
9. Was the duration of the first Wright Brothers flight over a minute?
10. What term used by allied pilots in WWII to describe UFO's was utilised by an American rock band formed in 1994?

FIND THE LINK (1) ANSWERS

1. SPAM
2. John PARROTT
3. ALBATROSS
4. LUMBERJACK
5. THE LIBERTY BELL
6. BRIAN Blessed
7. IDLE hands
8. SPANISH INQUISITION
9. PIRANHA
10. Sarah PALIN

LINK: MONTY PYTHON *(Spam sketch, Parrot sketch, Albatross sketch, I'm A Lumberjack song, The Liberty Bell title music, Life of Brian film, Eric Idle, Spanish Inquisition sketch, Piranha Brothers sketch, Michael Palin)*

PLANE CRAZY ANSWERS

1. NORTH BY NORTH WEST
2. KING KONG
3. THE RED ARROWS
4. LISA
5. THE 'RUSSIAN' SUPERSONIC TUPOLEV TU-144
6. BATTLE OF BRITAIN
7. THE DAM BUSTERS
8. CONCORDE
9. NO IT WAS 59 SECONDS
10. FOO FIGHTERS

Answer 7

UNIVERSALLY CHALLENGING

1. Which of the Teletubbies has a triangular antenna?

2. Who did frame Roger Rabbit?

3. Who was the Wombles cook?

4. Miriam Dervish, Vera Stanhope and Sister Ignatious are roles made famous by an actress awarded an OBE in 2003. Who is she?

5. What sort of shop can be found at 84 Charing Cross Road?

6. And who lived at 52 Festive Road, London?

7. In which country does Tom Hanks attempt to save Private Ryan?

8. As at 2019 the University of Manchester and Magdalen College, Oxford share a distinction on a long-running TV quiz. What is it?

9. What is a connection between the films *Ghost*, *Octopussy* and *10* ?

10. What connects The Vixen, The Sinnerman, The Governess, The Beast and The Dark Destroyer?

CONNECTIONS (4)

Answer the first 9 questions and find a connection for answer 10

1. Excluding re-elections to the post, who was the UK's 13th Prime Minister since the outbreak of World War II?

2. Which famous lyricist is also co-founder of the *Guinness Book of Hit Singles*?

3. Which former model and *Eastenders* actress, who rose to fame in a TV "booze advert", played Dolly Clothes-peg in *Worzel Gummidge*?

4. Which UK Olympic Gold medallist in two consecutive Games also broke the World Decathlon record four times?

5. In 1985, who duetted with Barbara Dickson in the song *I Know Him So Well* - still the best -selling record by a female duo?

6. In January 2009, which '80s pop star received a 15 months prison sentence on charges of false imprisonment?

7. Which music hall, television and film comedian, who died in 1990, was famous for his funny walks, deep sad voice and rubber faced gurns?

8. What was the name of Michael J Fox's character in the *Back To The Future* films?

9. Which comedian, who died in 1983, had his own series in which characters included Lampwick, Mandy and Clarence?

10. What connects all nine answers?

UNIVERSALLY CHALLENGING ANSWERS

1. **TINKY WINKY**
2. **JUDGE DOOM** *(played by Christopher Lloyd)*
3. **MADAME CHOLET**
4. **BRENDA BLETHYN** *(Outside Edge, Vera and The Calling)*
5. **A BOOK SHOP** *(1987 film)*
6. **MR BENN**
7. **FRANCE**
8. **MOST WINS ON UNIVERSITY CHALLENGE** ***4 TIMES***
9. **MOORE** *(Demi, Roger and Dudley)*
10. **ALL ARE CHASERS ON THE CHASE**

(Jenny Ryan, Paul Sinha, Anne Hegerty, Mark Labbett, Shaun Wallace)

Question 10

CONNECTIONS (4) ANSWERS

1. GORDON BROWN

2. TIM RICE

3. LORRAINE CHASE

4. DALEY THOMPSON

5. ELAINE PAIGE

6. BOY GEORGE

7. MAX WALL

8. MARTY McFLY

9. DICK EMERY

10. PAPER – ***brown, rice, chase, daily, page, boy, wall, McFly, & emery***

CRANIAL CHALLENGE

1. What was launched on TV in 1994 with the slogan 'It could be you'?

2. What fruit is the main ingredient of a traditional English Charlotte pudding?

3. Which official person resides in The Mansion House in London?

4. What was the first product to be advertised on British TV in 1955.

5. Which Division 3 Football team beat Arsenal 3 -1 in the 1969 League Cup Final at a muddy Wembley?

6. Which branch of the British armed forces march to the tune, *A Life on the Ocean Wave*?

7. In what subject at school would you have been taught the Binary system?

8. What was the name of the Cafe in the 1942 film classic *Casablanca?*

9. Which singer had 16 UK top 40 hits including *Dream Lover*, *Multiplication* and *Things*?

10. Look at the letters below. A phrase with vowels removed. Something a tennis umpire may say!

TECHNICOLOUR TRIVIA

1. What links a red wine from Bordeaux with Burnley and West Ham?

2. Which 1939 epic was the first colour film to win a best film Oscar?

3. Which Stephen King novel features a pet mouse named Mr Jingles?

4. Anthony Kiedis is an American musician best known as the lead singer of which band?

5. The Blue John Cavern is in which British national park?

6. What colour is the zero on a roulette wheel?

7. With which high street store would you associate Jacqueline Gold?

8. Who in 2012 gave birth to her daughter, Blue Ivy Carter?

9. The name of which colour is derived from the French word for 'mole' ?

10. In which 1968 animated film were the villains called Blue Meanies?

CRANIAL CHALLENGE ANSWERS

1. THE NATIONAL LOTTERY

2. APPLES

3. THE LORD MAYOR

Answer 4

4. GIBBS SR TOOTHPASTE

5. SWINDON TOWN

6. ROYAL MARINES

7. MATHS

8. RICKS CAFE

9. BOBBY DARIN

10. ISLAMABAD

TECHNICOLOUR TRIVIA ANSWERS

1. CLARET
2. GONE WITH THE WIND
3. THE GREEN MILE
4. THE RED HOT CHILLI PEPPERS
5. THE PEAK DISTRICT
6. GREEN
7. ANN SUMMERS
8. BEYONCE
9. TAUPE
10. YELLOW SUBMARINE

Answer 5

TIME FOR BED

1. In the animated television series *The Flintstones*, where did Fred and Wilma live?
A) Bedrock B) Bedminster C) Bedlam D) Bedford

2. Name the type of bed that is hinged at one end to store vertically against the wall or inside a closet or cabinet.

3. Which expression means 'To go to bed'? A) Hit the road B) Hit the sack C) Hit the floor

4. What type of rodent fell asleep in a teapot at the Mad Hatter's tea party in *Alice in Wonderland*?

5. Which singer had a hit with a Roger Cook / Bobby Wood song *Talking In Your Sleep in 1978?*

6. Who committed the murders in the film *A Nightmare On Elm Street* ?

7. Linked to Q1, who were the first couple in a TV series to be actually seen sharing a double bed?

8. What phobia is the fear of sleep? A) Alektorophobia B) Leukophobia C) Somniphobia

9. Which famous diarist would often conclude his daily entry with variants of "...and so to bed."?

10. Which talking jack-in-the-box with magical powers coined the phrase, 'Time for Bed'?

MAKE ME AN ISLAND

1. Which island with a population of just 28 *(2007)* is the largest island in the Bristol Channel?

2. Which fictional island is the setting for the shark attacks in the 1975 Spielberg film classic *Jaws* ?

3. In the Falklands war which island, invaded by Argentina, was the first British territory retaken in April 1982?

4. Which imaginary island is setting for the TV sitcom series *Father Ted*?

5. Which South Pacific island owned by Chile is home to statues dating to 1,100 and 1,500 CE? *(CE refers to the Common Era)*

6. On which invented island did the monster ape King Kong live?

7. Queen Victoria's Royal Residence, Osborne House, is on which island in the English Channel?

8. *Islands In The Stream, sung by a duo,* peaked at number 7 in the UK in 1983. Which renowned country singer who died in 2020 joined Dolly Parton on the vocals?

9. Port Moresby is the capital city of which southwestern Pacific island?

10. In which island group, off the UK, is the Bishop Rock lighthouse?

TIME FOR BED ANSWERS

1. A) BEDROCK
2. MURPHY BED
3. B) HIT THE SACK
4. A DORMOUSE
5. CRYSTAL GAYLE
6. FRED KREUGER
7. FRED AND WILMA FLINTSTONE
8. C) SOMNIPHOBIA
9. SAMUEL PEPYS
10. ZEBEDEE *(IN THE MAGIC ROUNDABOUT)*

Answer 7

MAKE ME AN ISLAND ANSWERS

1. LUNDY
2. AMITY
3. SOUTH GEORGIA
4. CRAGGY ISLAND
5. EASTER ISLAND
6. SKULL ISLAND
7. ISLE OF WIGHT
8. KENNY ROGERS
9. PAPUA NEW GUINEA
10. SCILLY ISLES

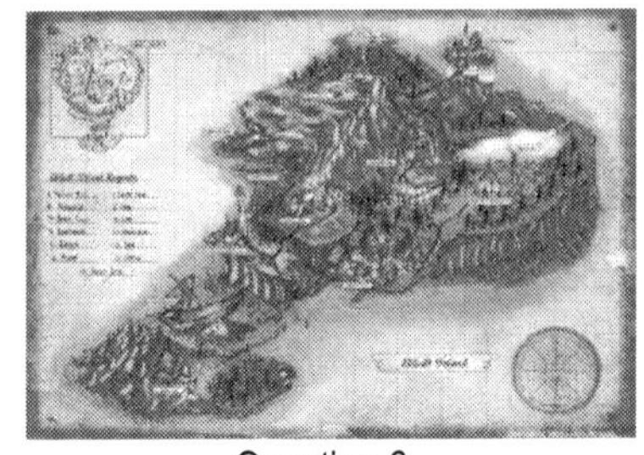
Question 6

WORDS AND NUMBERS (2)

1. What is Blue John? A) Rude comedian B) Jazz Singer C) Semi precious mineral *(1pt)*

2. How many lines in a Limerick? A) 5 B) 7 C) 9 *(1pt)*

3. If you dial 123 on a BT phone, what will you hear?
   A. Speaking Clock B. Weather C. Directory enquiries *(2pts)*

4. Which Nervous Breakdown did The Rolling Stones sing about in 1966?
A) 13th B) 18th C)19th *(2pts)*

5. What Type of Fruit is a Persian Apple? A) Peach B) Peach C) Pomegranate *(3pts)*

6. Including wisdom teeth, how many teeth does a fully-grown adult have? A) 28 B) 30 C) 32 *(3pts)*

7. What kind of structure was the ancient Pharos at Alexandria?
   A) Lighthouse B) Temple C) Pyramid *(4pts)*

8. What is the measurement distance of an Olympic Veloderome Track?
   A) 200 metres B. 250 metres C. 400 metres *(4pts)*

9. What type of creature is a Tarantula Hawk?
   A) Wasp B) Moth C) Dragon Fly *(5pts)*

10. Which Song was ABBA's last UK Number 1?
    A) Take A Chance On Me B) Super Trouper C) Winner Takes it All *(5pts)*

EXTENDED ROUND (3)
TINA TURNER

An extended round is great to add variety to a quiz night. Sheets are handed out at the beginning of the quiz and answers have to be completed at a later stage of the quiz - quite often the half-time break. Often this takes the form of a Picture Round. However there are other options. This round is a simple job of listing as many nominated hits as you can within a specified time. See the instruction below. The complete list of possible answers is shown on the following page. Good luck.

*Name as many of the Top 40 Hits of **TINA TURNER** as you can in 10 minutes!*

WORDS AND NUMBERS (2) ANSWERS

1. C) SEMI PRECIOUS MINERAL - *1 point*

2. A) 5 -*1 point*

3. A) SPEAKING CLOCK - *2 points*

4. C) 19TH - *2 points*

5. B) PEACH - *3 points*

6. C) 32 - *3 points*

7. A) LIGHTHOUSE - *4 points*

8. B) 250 METRES - *4 points*

9. A) WASP - *5 points*

10. B) SUPER TROUPER - *5 points*

EXTENDED ROUND (3) ANSWERS
TINA TURNER

BE TENDER WITH ME BABY
THE BEST
DISCO INFERNO
GOLDENEYE
HELP
I DON'T WANNA FIGHT
I DON'T WANNA LOSE YOU
I WANT YOU NEAR ME
IN YOUR WILDEST DREAMS
LET'S STAY TOGETHER
LOOK ME IN THE HEART
LOVE THING
MISSING YOU
NUTBUSH CITY LIMITS
ON SILENT WINGS
OPEN ARMS
PRIVATE DANCER
SOMETHING BEAUTIFUL
REMAINS
STEAMY WINDOWS
TYPICAL MALE
WAY OF THE WORLD
WE DON'T NEED ANOTHER
HERO (THUNDERDOME)
WHAT YOU SEE IS WHAT YOU SEE
WHATEVER YOU WANT
WHATEVER YOU NEED
WHAT'S LOVE GOT TO DO WITH IT
WHEN THE HEARTACHE IS OVER
WHY MUST WE WAIT UNTIL TONIGHT

BLOCKBUSTERS (3)

1. Which **TT** in The Supermarionation series is the Captain of *Stingray*?

2. What **B** was a pen name used by Charles Dickens?

3. The Titanic set sail from Southampton on the 10th April 1912 what **C** was its next port of call?

4. What **BOM** won the Eurovision song contest for the UK in 1976?

5. What **AL** are the two middle names of Prince George?

6. What **IGONOI** was the slogan used in a Wickes TV advertisement?

7. What **AI** is an organisation whose logo is a candle wrapped in barbed wire?

8. What **GH** composed the orchestral *Planets Suite*?

9. What **TCOM** is a 1986 film with the Characters Fast Eddie Felson and Vincent Lauria?

10. What **CYFTLT** is a song from the musical *The Lion King* ?

ROUND ROBIN

The last letter of the 1st answer is the first letter of the 2nd answer and so on. Question 10's last letter is the first letter of Q1 to complete the circle

1. What is the Medical name for your Breast bone.

2. Which Actor played Col.Steiner in the Film *The Eagle Has Landed.*

3. By what name is a person known who is appointed to carry out a deceased person's affairs.

4. Who did Hitler appoint as the Nazi Party Foreign Minister in 1938 – 1945.

5. In which TV series did Angie Dickinson play – Sgt. Pepper Anderson.

6. What is the Chemical name for Laughing Gas.

7. What name connects an Alpine flower and a song from *Sound of Music*

8. What is the most common surname in Scotland.

9. Which County Cricket club play home at The Rose Bowl.

10. Name the REM song later released as a charity single by Helping Haiti that reached number 1 in 2010 to aid the victims of the earthquake.

BLOCKBUSTERS (3) ANSWERS

1. TROY TEMPEST
2. BOZ
3. CHERBOURG
4. BROTHERHOOD OF MAN
5. ALEXANDER LOUIS
6. ITS GOT OUR NAME ON IT
7. AMNESTY INTERNATIONAL
8. GUSTAV HOLST

9. THE COLOUR OF MONEY
10. CAN YOU FEEL THE LOVE TONIGHT

ROUND ROBIN ANSWERS

1. STERNUM
2. MICHAEL CAINE
3. EXECUTOR
4. RIBBENTROP
5. POLICEWOMAN
6. NITROUS OXIDE

7. EDLEWIESS
8. SMITH
9. HAMPSHIRE
10. EVERYBODY HURTS

SPOT THE DOG!

Just name these 10 famous canines

RIDDLE:

You have me today, Tomorrow you'll have more; As your time passes, I'm not easy to store; I don't take up space, But I'm only in one place; I am what you saw, But not what you see. What am I?

SPOT THE DOG! ANSWERS

1. **PUDSEY** (Won Britain's Got Talent in 2012 with owner Ashleigh Butler)

2. **MUTTLEY** (Wacky Races)

3. **TOTO** (Wizard of Oz)

4. **SCOOBY DOO** (Where are you!)

5. **SHEP** (Blue Peter with John Craven)

6. **GROMIT** (Wallace & Gromit)

7. **LASSIE** (Heroine of many films)

8. **GREYFRIARS BOBBY** (Edinburgh statue)

GREYFRIARS BOBBY (May 4, 1855 – January 14, 1872) was a Skye Terrier who became known in 19th-century Edinburgh for spending 14 years guarding the grave of his owner until he died himself on 14 January 1872. The story continues to be well known in Scotland, through several books and films. A prominent commemorative statue and nearby graves are a tourist attraction.

The best-known version of the story is that Bobby belonged to John Gray, who worked for the Edinburgh City Police as a nightwatchman. When John Gray died he was buried in Greyfriars Kirkyard, the kirkyard surrounding Greyfriars Kirk in the Old Town of Edinburgh. Bobby then became known locally, spending the rest of his life sitting on his master's grave.

9. **NIPPER** (Bristol born star of HMV record labels)

10. **DOUGAL** (Magic Roundabout)

RIDDLE ANSWER

MEMORIES

THINK CAREFULLY NOW!

1. Where is Davy Jones Locker?

2. Which flower gets its name from a mythological character who fell in love with his reflection?

3. What substance used by painters in DIY & the building trade is made from linseed oil & chalk?

4. What is the only bird that can fly backwards?

5. Which Composer was known as the Waltz King. *The Blue Danube* waltz being one of his compositions?

6. In TV's *Only Fools & Horses*, what name does Trigger call Rodney?

7. Which Famous authors pen name was Boz?

8. If you see LBV on a bottle of Port what does it stand for?

9. Who was Head Coach for the 2017 British & Irish Rugby Union tour to New Zealand.

10. Which 17th century poet wrote *Paradise Lost* and *Paradise Regained*?

ITALIANA

1. What was the currency of Italy before it changed to the Euro?
2. What is the name of the famous Renaissance church in The Vatican?
3. Which animal provides the milk for the hard Italian cheese Pecorino?
4. Which well known Puccini aria was used by the BBC as its theme for the 1990 World Cup?
5. Which Italian island was the first place of exile for Napoleon?
6. The Italian number Ventuno is the equivalent of what in English?
7. Once a thriving and sophisticated Roman city what is now a vast archaeological site in southern Italy's Campania region, near the coast of the Bay of Naples?

8. In the 2003 remake of The Italian Job, who played Charlie Croker, the role made famous by Michael Caine in the 1969 original?

9. Which 13th/14th century explorer, with links to Bristol, made long trips of discovery along the silk road to Asia and China?

10. In which year were the Summer Olympics held in Rome?

THINK CAREFULLY NOW! ANSWERS

1. BOTTOM OF THE SEA

2. NARCISSUS

3. PUTTY

4. HUMMING BIRD

5. JOHANN STRAUSS

6. DAVE.

7. CHARLES DICKENS.

8. LATE BOTTLED VINTAGE..

9. WARREN GATLAND..

10. JOHN MILTON.

ITALIANA ANSWERS

1. LIRA

2. ST PETERS BASILICA

3. EWE - SHEEP

4. NESSUN DORMA

5. ELBA

6. 21

7. POMPEII

Answer 7

8. MARK WAHLBERG

9. MARCO POLO

10. 1960

PROGRESSION

Multi choice questions worth increasing points as you progress!

1. In a standard double 6 game of dominoes how many tiles are used? A) 24 B) 28 C) 32 ***(1pt)***

2. Who performed the song Jack In The Box for the UK in the 1971 Eurovision Song Contest. It came 4th and reached No 4 in the charts? A) Sandie Shaw B) Lulu C) Clodagh Rodgers ***(1pt)***

3. How much was the first combined TV & Radio licence in 1946? A) 10s B) £1 C) £2 ***(2pts)***

4. In 1981 Susan Brown became the first sportswoman to do which of these:
A) Cox the Boat Race B) Ride the National C) Climb Everest ***(2pts)***

5. What does a deltiologist study? A) Rivers B) Postcards C) Aircraft ***(3pt)***

6. In the final episode of Dad's Army who did Corporal Jones marry?
A) Mrs Setter B) Mrs Goose C) Mrs Fox ***(3pts)***

7. Which king was the oldest when he succeeded to the throne?
A) George IV B) Edward VIII C) William IV ***(4pts)***

8. How many acres are in a square mile? A) 440 B) 540 C) 640 ***(4pts)***

9. What is a California Zephyr? A) Warm Pacific wind B) Passenger train C) Desert lizard ***(5pts)***

10. The Pintapi tribe who first came into contact with white people in 1985 are from which continent?
A) Australia B) South America C) Africa ***(5pts)***

I DON'T BELIEVE IT!

1. What is the collective name for a group of unicorns?

2. The UK's Dyslexia Research Trust is based in which city?

3. It is illegal in Texas to put what on your neighbour's cow?

4. Henry VIII introduced which tax into England in 1535?

5. What is the most popular colour for toilet paper in France?

6. What were the first ice hockey pucks made from?

7. True or False? You can sneeze in your sleep!

8. In what country are there 6 villages called Silly, 12 called Billy and 2 called Pratt?

9. What bird is nicknamed The Laughing Jackass?

10. Who invented the word vomit?

PROGRESSION ANSWERS

1. B) 28

2. C) CLODAGH RODGERS

3. C) £2

4. A) COX THE BOAT RACE (*OXFORD WON BY 8 LENGTHS)*

5. B) POSTCARDS

6. C) MRS FOX

7. C) WILLIAM IV

8. C) 640

9. B) PASSENGER TRAIN

10. A) AUSTRALIA

I DON'T BELIEVE IT! ANSWERS

1. A BLESSING
2. READING
3. GRAFFITI
4. A BEARD TAX
5. PINK
6. FROZEN COW DUNG
7. FALSE
8. FRANCE
9. KOOKABURRA
10. WILLIAM SHAKESPEARE

Answer 3

TICKLISH ALLSORTS

1. What word connects lantern, marker, mushroom and flute?

2. A statue of which cartoon character adorns Crystal City, Texas, the Spinach Capital of the World?

3. In 1948 Pierre Boulanger built which model car that could accommodate a French farmer, his pig and his bowler hat?

4. Who won her first Grammy award in 1999 after 16 years in the pop business?

5. What is the perfect score in a game of ten-pin bowling?

6. Name the wild west character in the who appeared between 1937 and 2003 in *The Dandy* comic whose favourite meal was cow pie?

7. Do bananas have seeds?

8. What is the capital of Tasmania?

9. According to *The Beatles* song *Penny Lane*, what photographs does the barber sell?

10. In what country are the Taurus Mountains?

MUSIC CHALLENGE

1. Who was nicknamed the *King of Skiffle* and influenced many 1960s British pop & rock musicians?

2. What do the initials EMI stand for?

3. *Any Dream Will Do* was a No1 hit for Jason Donovan in 1991 and a No2 for Lee Mead in 2007. For what 1968 show was the song written?

4. Who was the writer of *Blue Suede Shoes* who died in 1999 aged 65?

5. The title of which 1973 No 4 hit for Elton John shares its name with a book of the Bible?

6. What was the title of the hugely successful 1995 third studio album by Alanis Morissette which reached number 1 in 13 countries?

7. The stunning flip side of *Life In The Fast Lane* by *The Eagles* tells of how man inevitably destroys the places he finds beautiful. Title please.

8. Who is missing from this group – a Native American, an American Policeman, a cowboy, a GI and a biker?

9. What name is given to half a quaver?

10. In which decade did cassette tapes go on sale?

TICKLISH ALLSORTS ANSWERS

1. MAGIC
2. POPEYE
3. CITROEN 2CV
4. MADONNA
5. 300
6. DESPERATE DAN

7. YES
8. HOBART
9. 'EVERY HEAD HE HAS HAD THE PLEASURE TO KNOW'
10. TURKEY

MUSIC CHALLENGE ANSWERS

1. LONNIE DONEGAN
2. ELECTRIC AND MUSICAL INDUSTRIES
3. JOSEPH AND THE AMAZING TECHNICOLOR DREAMCOAT
4. CARL PERKINS
5. DANIEL
6. JAGGED LITTLE PILL
7. THE LAST RESORT

Answer 8

8. A CONSTRUCTION WORKER - *VILLAGE PEOPLE (YMCA ETC) OUTFITS*
9. SEMI-QUAVER?
10. THE 1960S

FOOTBALL FROLICS

1. In what colour do the New Zealand football international team play?

2. Founded by two clergymen, what is London's oldest football club?

3. Which 71 year old ex footballer and manager won *I'm a Celebrity...Get Me Out of Here!* In 2018 and was crowned *King of the Jungle* ?

4. What sort of animal was World Cup Willie, England's 1966 mascot?

5. Chelsea's Peter Osgood was the last player to achieve what feat in the FA Cup?

6. Which soccer team shared its name with a novel by Sir Walter Scott?

7. In the 1986 World Cup finals, who was sent off while captaining England?

8. As at March 2020 who holds the record number of appearances for the England women's national football team?

9. Who was the youngest member of England's World Cup winning team in 1966?

10. Which footballing nation won its first ever competitive game in 1990 when they beat Austria?

TARTAN TEASERS

1. What is Scotland's national animal?

2. Donald Trump's mother was born in the village of Crathie. On which Scottish island?

3. Which language became an official language of Scotland in 2005?

4. What is the largest (in area) freshwater loch (or lake) in Scotland?

5. What is the approximate population of Scotland?

6. What sort of lift is the famous rotating Falkirk Wheel?

7. Can you name the 19th-century Skye Terrier who became famous for spending 14 years guarding the grave of his owner?

8. Which king ruled Scotland from 1040 to his death in battle in 1057?

9. At the Battle of Culloden, how many of the Royal Troops were killed altogether?

10. When he died in 1329, Robert the Bruce's body was buried next to his wife in Dunfermline Abbey. Where, however, was his heart buried?

FOOTBALL FROLICS ANSWERS

1. ALL WHITE

2. FULHAM

3. HARRY REDKNAPP

4. A LION

5. SCORED IN EVERY ROUND *INC REPLAYED FINAL*

6. HEART OF MIDLOTHIAN

7. RAY WILKINS

8. FARA WILLIAMS *(40 goals)*

9. ALAN BALL

10. FAROE ISLANDS

Answer 3

TARTAN TEASERS ANSWERS

1. THE UNICORN

2. ISLE OF LEWIS

3. GAELIC

4. LOCH LOMOND

5. 5,119,200 *(IN 1999)*

6. A BOAT LIFT

7. GREYFRIARS BOBBY

8. MACBETH

9. 50

10, MELROSE ABBEY *(BODY IN DUNFERMLINE ABBEY)*

Answer 6

QUIZ OF QUIZZES

1. For geography questions, new contestants on *Pointless* are briefed: "If in doubt, say..."?

2. The creator of *Mastermind* based the show on a recurrent nightmare in which he re-lived what experience?

3. *University Challenge* was based on a US quiz which featured soldiers instead of students. Its famous phrases, "starters for ten" and "bonuses" were taken from which sport?

4. For how long did Kevin Ashman appear on *Eggheads* before his first incorrect answer to a history question?

5. Charles Ingram, was disqualified for cheating on *Who Wants To Be A Millionaire*. Two years later, his episode was finally shown. What was the first (somewhat appropriate) advert shown in the first break?

6. Lionel Blair and Una Stubbs were the original team captains on which charades based game show?

7. Who hosted the cerebral & action quiz *The Krypton Factor*?

8. What was the booby prize on *3-2-1*?

9. Can you name the three hosts of *Blankety Blank*?

10. What TV quiz was hosted by Anne Widdecombe?

IT'S NOT ALL IN THE MIND!

1. Which English singer/songwriter/guitarist's hits include *Shotgun*, *Budapest* & *Blame It On Me*?

2. Which English Test Cricketer took 8 Aussie wickets for 25 runs at Trent Bridge in August 2015?

3. *The Birthday Party* and *The Caretaker* are works by which playwright?

4. What event in 1666 is estimated to have destroyed the homes of 70,000 of the city's 80,000 inhabitants?

5. Which outer part of your body has the medical term Pollux?

6. The natural phenomenon *Aurora Borealis* is also known by what name?

7. Which bank is credited with opening the first 'Hole in the Wall' machine, now sadly disappearing from many locations around the country?

8. Who played the part of Ethan Hunt in the *Mission Impossible* films?

9. Vodka is the alcoholic content of a Bloody Mary. Which spirit is used in a Bloody Maria?

10. By surface area which is the smallest of the North American Great Lakes?

QUIZ OF QUIZZES ANSWERS

1. CENTRAL AFRICAN REPUBLIC

2. BEING INTERROGATED AS A NAZI P-O-W

3. BASKETBALL

4. 10 YEARS 1 MONTH 27 DAYS

5. BENYLIN COUGH MIXTURE

6. GIVE US A CLUE

7. GORDON BURNS

8. DUSTY BIN

9. TERRY WOGAN, LES DAWSON AND LILY SAVAGE

10. CLEVERDICKS

IT'S NOT ALL IN THE MIND! ANSWERS

1. GEORGE EZRA

2. STUART BROAD

3. HAROLD PINTER

4. THE GREAT FIRE OF LONDON

5. THUMB

6. THE NORTHERN LIGHTS

7. BARCLAYS

8. TOM CRUISE

9. TEQUILA

10. ONTARIO

CONNECTIONS (5)

1. Who drove the Turbo Terrific in the *Wacky Races* cartoon?
2. In the book *Treasure Island,* what was the name of the ship in which Jim Hawkins sailed?
3. Standing on the site of Newgate Prison, what is the nickname of London's Central Criminal Court?
4. What was the title of John Wayne's last film?
5. Opened in 1889, which famous Parisian nightspot is in the Jardin de Paris, Montmartre Hill?
6. What scientific name did Galileo Galilei give to the Northern Lights?
7. Established in 1887, where is the famous Raffles Hotel?
8. First published in 1928, the title character of which famous novel is named Constance?
9. What name is given to someone who makes barrels?
10. What connects all nine answers?

TUNED TO THE CLASSICS

1. Which conductor always appeared on the podium wearing a white carnation?

2. Who wrote a piece called the *Skittle Alley Trio* ?

3. The Hallelujah Chorus comes from which work, often performed at Christmas?

4. Pomp & Circumstance March No 1 by Sir Edward William Elgar is better known as what?

5. Which composer was able to write, despite becoming almost totally deaf in later life?

6. What term is used to describe a composition in which one or more solo instruments are assigned leading roles, often with orchestral accompaniment?

7. Which of these instruments is not included in a standard string quartet?
A) Double Bass B) Viola C) Cello D) Violin

8. In which keyboard instrument would a plectrum be found?
A) Fortepiano B) Clavichord C) Piano D) Harpsichord

9. Symphony No 9 in E minor is popularly known as the 'New World Symphony'. Who composed it?

10. *Largo al factotum* is an aria sung by the title character from which opera?

CONNECTIONS (5) ANSWERS

1. PETER PERFECT
2. THE HISPANIOLA
3. THE OLD BAILEY
4. THE SHOOTIST
5. THE MOULIN ROUGE
6. AURORA BOREALIS
7. SINGAPORE
8. LADY CHATTERLEY'S LOVER
9. COOPER

10. HIDDEN ANIMAL/BIRD SOUNDS

(purr, hiss, bay, hoot, moo, roar, sing, chatter, coo)

TUNED TO THE CLASSICS ANSWERS

1. SIR MALCOLM SARGENT
2. WOLFGANG AMADEUS MOZART
3. THE MESSIAH
4. LAND OF HOPE AND GLORY
5. LUDWIG VAN BEETHOVEN
6. CONCERTO
7. A) DOUBLE BASS
8. D) HARPSICHORD
9. ANTONIN DVORAK
10. THE BARBER OF SEVILLE

Answer 8

EXTENDED ROUND (4)
THE ROLLING STONES

An extended round is great to add variety to a quiz night. Sheets are handed out at the beginning of the quiz and answers have to be completed at a later stage of the quiz - quite often the half-time break. Often this takes the form of a Picture Round. However there are other options. This round is a simple job of listing as many nominated hits as you can within a specified time. See the instruction below. The complete list of possible answers is shown on the following page. Good luck.

Name as many of the Top 20 Hits of
THE ROLLING STONES
as you can in 10 minutes!

THE LETTER M

1. What cocktail of whisky and vermouth is named after one of the five boroughs of New York?

2. What was the former name of Snickers chocolate bar in the UK?

3. Which Royal Navy rank comes between cadet and sub-lieutenant?

4. What is the medical name for the lower jaw bone?

5. What name is shared by a small orange and a Chinese official?

6. Which Beatles song was taken to number one in the UK by The Overlanders?

7. Which mythological beast was killed by Theseus?

8. What is the male equivalent of a mermaid?

9. Which game of Chinese origin is played with 144 rectangular tiles?

10. What is the name of a trader who sells silk and woollen cloth?

EXTENDED ROUND (4) ANSWERS
THE ROLLING STONES

ANGIE
BITCH
BROWN SUGAR
DANDELION
EMOTIONAL RESCUE
FAR AWAY EYES
FOOL TO CRY
GET OFF MY CLOUD
HARLEM SHUFFLE
HAVE YOU SEEN YOUR MOTHER BABY STANDING IN THE SHADOW
HONKY TONK WOMEN
(I CAN'T GET NO) SATISFACTION
I WANNA BE YOUR MAN
IT'S ALL OVER NOW
IT'S ONLY ROCK AND ROLL
JUMPING JACK FLASH
THE LAST TIME
LET IT ROCK
LET'S SPEND THE NIGHT TOGETHER
LIKE A ROLLING STONE
LITTLE RED ROOSTER
LOVE IS STRONG
MISS YOU
NINETEENTH NERVOUS BREAKDOWN
NOT FADE AWAY
PAINT IT BLACK
ROUGH JUSTICE
RUBY TUESDAY
START ME UP
STREETS OF LOVE

THE LETTER M ANSWERS

1. MANHATTAN
2. MARATHON
3. MIDSHIPMAN
4. MANDIBLE
5. MANDARIN
6. MICHELLE
7. MINOTAUR
8. MERMAN
9. MAHJONG
10. MERCER

Answer 7

WORDS AND NUMBERS (3)

1. Which of these is an ABBA song? A) Waterloo B) Peekaboo C Vindaloo ***(1pt)***

2. Which one of these numbers is not a scoring value in Scrabble? A) 4 B) 5 C) 6 ***(1pt)***

3. What animal is a white faced Dartmoor? A) Cattle B) Sheep C) Pony ***(2pts)***

4. In Harry Potter the Hogwarts Houses are Ravenclaw, Gryffindor & Slytherin. What is the fourth?
A) Huffenpuff B) Hufflepuff C) Hufferpuffer ***(2pts)***

5. Thailand was formerly known by which name? A. Siam B) Laos C) Borneo ***(3pts)***

6. A sackbut is an early form of which musical instrument? A) Clarinet B) Trombone C) Tuba ***(3pts)***

7. In Rugby Union what position is usually occupied by the No 6 shirt?
A) Prop B Openside Flanker C Blindside Flanker ***(4pts)***

8. Who was the first senior UK Royal Family member to appear on the cover of Vogue?
A) Princess Anne B) Princess Diana C). Sarah Ferguson ***(4pts)***

9. Which Bingo call is Heaven's Gate? A) 58 B) 68 C) 78 ***(5pts)***

10. Eructation is a medical term for what condition? A) Burping B) Hiccups C) Sneezing ***(5pts)***

FULL CIRCLE

Last letter of Ans 1 to Q1 is 1st letter of Q2 and so on. Last letter of Q10 will be 1st letter of Q1

1. What was the name of the girlfriend shot dead by Paralympic champion Oscar Pistorius in 2013?

2. By what name is the female reproductive part of a Flower known?

3. In the novel *Gullivers Travels* what was the name of the land of tiny people that shipwrecked Gulliver is washed up on.

4. Name the operational system of 4 Vanguard-class submarines armed with D-5 ballistic missiles that began patrols in 1994?

5. In William Shakespeare's *Midsummer Nights Dream,* who is the Queen of the Fairies?

6. Little Rock is the capital of which US state?

7. Which 1960 Film stars Kirk Douglas as a slave who rebels against the Romans?

8. In Harness Racing what is the name of the 2 wheeled cart pulled by the horse?

9. Which is Canada's western most territory that borders Alaska?

10. Name the English band with a string of hits between 1981 and 2010, then linked to England football team for a number 1 in 1990.

WORDS AND NUMBERS (3) ANSWERS

1. A) WATERLOO - *1 point*

2. C) 6 - *1 point*

Answer 6

3. B) SHEEP - *2 points*

4. B) HUFFLEPUFF- *2 points*

5. A) SIAM - *3 points*

6. B) TROMBONE - *3 points*

7. C) BLINDSIDE FLANKER - *4 points*

8. A) PRINCESS ANNE - *4 points*

9. C) 78 - *5 points*

10. A) BURPING - *5 points*

FULL CIRCLE CIRCLES ANSWERS

1. REEVA STEENKAMP

2. PISTIL

3. LILLIPUT

4. TRIDENT

5. TITANIA

6. ARKANSAS

Answer 6

7. SPARTACUS

8. SULKY

9. YUKON

10. NEW ORDER

QUESTIONS, QUESTIONS

1. Both Sir Edward Elgar and Adam Smith have featured on which British banknote?
2. **FILCH THE BONELESS MEAT** is an anagram of what major movie?
3. Dustbin lid and Lion's Mane are what types of creature?
4. Apparently Burnley FC sells the most of what on each match day at Turf Moor?
   a) Pies b) Beer c) Benedictine Liqueur
5. Lina Lamont and Don Lockwood are characters in which musical?
6. What word connects a German wine and part of a horse's leg?
7. Which author wrote the Tilly Trotter and Mary Ann series of novels?
8. Eleanor of Aquitane was Consort to which English King from 1154 to 1189?
9. From which country does Emmental cheese originate?
10. What type of product gets its name from its inventor Clarice Cliff?

THE LETTER C

1. Name the building in which the American Congress meets.

2. What type of animal tried vainly to catch Roadrunner in Warner Brothers cartoons?

3. Which British rock band took *Viva La Vida* to number one in 2008?

4. Which series of horror films began with a single mother giving her son a much sought-after doll for his birthday, only to discover that it is possessed by the soul of a serial killer?

5. Which American state has the highest population?

6. What links the British Prime Minister's country residence with a Chinese strategy board game of German origin?

7. Name the do-it-yourself home improvement TV show broadcast in the UK on BBC between 1996 and 2004.

8. Who is missing: Heath, Wilson, ??????, Thatcher?

9. Where was the site of the battle in 1746, where British troops finally defeated the Scottish Jacobite army near Inverness?

10. What is the 1977 American science fiction film directed by Steven Spielberg upon which the title of this book is adapted?

QUESTIONS, QUESTIONS.... ANSWERS

1. £20 NOTE

2. THE SILENCE OF THE LAMBS

3. JELLYFISH

Answer 9

C) BENEDICTINE LIQUEUR

5. SINGING IN THE RAIN

6. HOCK

7. CATHERINE COOKSON

8. HENRY II

9. SWITZERLAND

10. POTTERY, CHINA

THE LETTER C ANSWERS

1. CAPITOL
2. COYOTE
3. COLDPLAY
4. CHILD'S PLAY
5. CALIFORNIA
6. CHEQUERS
7. CHANGING ROOMS
8. CALLAGHAN
9. CULLODEN
10. CLOSE ENCOUNTERS OF THE THIRD KIND

Answer 2

FOUR DIRECTIONS

1. What was the product advertised on TV with the slogan 'Full of Eastern promise'?

2. In 1982 which island was invaded by Argentina, starting the Falklands War?

3. On a mariner's compass, what point is between due west and south west?

4. Which US Vietnam veteran was convicted and later cleared of charges relating to the Iran/Contra arms affair in 1989?

5. Beginning in February 2018 and continuing into March, by what name was the severe, cold weather in the UK, dubbed by the Met Office?

6. Who played Batman in the 1960s TV series?

7. Who wrote the novel *Northanger Abbey*?

8. Which seaside resort has the longest pier in the UK extending 2.16 kilometres into the Thames Estuary?

9. Name the large market town and the county town in the East Midlands that lies on the River Nene and is famous for shoe-making.

10. Which Scottish Championship football club, based in Dumfries, is mentioned in the Gospels of Matthew and Luke in the Bible?

BLOCKBUSTERS (4)

1. What **JW** is the Archbishop of Canterbury?

2. What **CT** stands on the top of Brandon Hill in Bristol?

3. What **IWLAAC** is a famous poem written by William Wordsworth?

4. What does the **PO** stand for in the P & O Cruise ship company?

5. Which **TAYRRTOOT** is a song containing the line, "I'm coming home I've done time now I've got know what is and isn't mine" ?

6. What **C** is the country residence retreat of the British P.M?

7. What **T** is a Roman Emperor and Star Trek's Captain Kirk's middle name?

8. What **FV** are the two words inscribed on a Victoria Cross?

9. What **TPM** is a line of 0 degrees longitude that runs through Greenwich?

10. What **WKAB** were on old time British music hall act who performed the Sand Dance.

FOUR DIRECTIONS ANSWERS

1. TURKISH DELIGHT
2. SOUTH GEORGIA
3. WEST SOUTH WEST
4. OLIVER NORTH
5. THE BEAST FROM THE EAST
6. ADAM WEST
7. JANE AUSTEN
8. SOUTHEND ON SEA
9. NORTHAMPTON
10. QUEEN OF THE SOUTH

Answer 6

BLOCKBUSTERS (4) ANSWERS

1. JUSTIN WELBY
2. CABOT TOWER
3. I WANDERED LONELY AS A CLOUD.
4. PENINSULAR & ORIENTAL.
5. TIE A YELLOW RIBBON ROUND THE OLD OAK TREE.
6. CHEQUERS.
7. TIBERIUS.
8. FOR VALOUR.
9. THE PRIME MERIDIAN.
10. WILSON, KEPPLE AND BETTY.

Answer 2

ONE

Every answer contains ONE

1. In the Wild West which Town did the shootout at OK Corral take place?

2. What word can be a old time sailing ship or a large Sherry glass?

3. Which South East Asian country is an archipelago made up of over 17 thousand islands and was known as the Dutch East Indies before WW 2?

4. The Jewish festival Yom Kippur is also known as The Day of what ?

5. Which 19th century Liberal politician held the post of Prime Minister 4 times?

6. What name is given to a small simple crown or decorative band worn by lesser royalty?

7. After the TV show *Not The 9 O'clock News* which Welsh comedian and actor formed a comedy partnership with the late Mel Smith?

8. Which highly fragrant climbing garden shrub is also known by the name Woodbine?

9. Which song contains these lines 'Does your memory stray to brighter sunny day. When I kissed you and called you sweetheart'?

10. What name is given to a puppet worked by from above by strings attached to its joints?

HISTORICAL QUEST

1. 1865, 1881, 1901..... What comes next?

2. Which English king was brutally murdered in Berkeley Castle, Gloucestershire in 1312?

3. What month and what year? The Grand Hotel, Brighton was bombed by the IRA and Indira Gandhi was assassinated.

4. In what year was Britain's only recorded earthquake fatality - when a man was hit by falling masonry from a London church? A) 1880 B) 1780 C) 1680 D) 1580

5. Who toured the streets of 19th century London, rescuing street boys and housing them?

6. Which king of England watched in dismay as his finest ship went down in battle on the Solent in 1545?

7. Who did Queen Elizabeth I knight on his return home in 1580?

8. Who was known as 'the iron duke'?

9. What left London's Waterloo station at 8.23 on 14 November 1994?

10. Who was the first British queen to have a living centenarian mother?

ONE ANSWERS

1. TOMBSTONE

2. SCHOONER.

3. INDONESIA

4. ATONEMENT

Answer 5

5. GLADSTONE

6. CORONET.

7. GRIFF RHYS-JONES.

8. HONEY SUCKLE.

9. ARE YOU LONESOME TONIGHT.

10. MARIONETTE

HISTORICAL QUEST ANSWERS

1. **1963** *(Years in which US presidents were assassinated)*

2. EDWARD II

Answer 2

3. 1984

4. D) 1580

5. DR BARNARDO

6. HENRY VIII

7. SIR FRANCIS DRAKE ***(after sailing around the world)***

8. THE DUKE OF WELLINGTON

9. THE EUROSTAR ***(FIRST COMMERCIAL JOURNEY)***

10. QUEEN ELIZABETH II

COMMERCIAL BREAK

Name the products advertised on television

LYRICS

From which songs do the following lyrics come and who sung them?

1. And I was thinking to myself this could be Heaven or this could be Hell
2. 'Cause you know I love the players and you love the game
3. Will you still be sending me a Valentine/ Birthday greetings bottle of wine?
4. She played the fiddle in an Irish band but she fell in love with an English man
5. You know I'm just a fool who's willing to sit around and wait for you.

COMMERCIAL BREAK ANSWERS

1. THE A.A

2. GO COMPARE

3. PG TIPS TEA

4. SMASH

5. COMPARE THE MARKET

6. ALDI

7. YELLOW PAGES

8. SKITTLES

9. BUD LIGHT BEER

10. WARBURTON'S BAGELS

LYRICS ANSWERS

1. HOTEL CALIFORNIA BY THE EAGLES

2. BLANK SPACE BY TAYLOR SWIFT

3. WHEN I'M 64 BY THE BEATLES

4. GALWAY GIRL BY ED SHEERAN

Don Felder & Joe Walsh of Eagles

5. HOPELESSLY DEVOTED TO YOU BY OLIVIA NEWTON-JOHN

COMETH THE AXEMEN!

1. What was peculiar about the way Jim Hendrix played his guitar, making him difficult to emulate?

2. Glam rock star Marc Bolan played a Fender Stratocaster on hits like *Get It On*. What was the name of the group with whom Marc played?

3. Ritchie Blackmore started his career as a session guitarist and played in several forgotten bands before finding success with which band?

4. David Gilmour succeeded which other guitar legend to bePink Floyd's lead guitarist in 1968?

5. What year was Stevie Ray Vaughan tragically killed in a helicopter at just 35 years of age?

6. Name the guitarist, widely imitated at the height of his fame, who had a distinctive and instantly recognisable sound with fluid use of the tremolo arm usually using a red Fender Stratocaster?

7. Which of these bands has not had significant use of Jimmy Page's great talent? A) Led Zeppelin B) Pearl Jam C) Cream D) The Yardbirds

8. Slow Hand' is the nickname of this legend and also the title of one of his albums featuring 'Wonderful Tonight' and Cocaine.' Who is he?

9. Former Marty Wilde & Wildcats guitarist, best known as a session guitarist he performed on around 750 chart singles over his career, including 54 UK Number One hits. Who was he?

10. Which English guitarist, known for finger-style and hybrid picking style, has worked with many top musicians from a wide range of genres in the studio and on tour, including the Everly Brothers?

WORDS AND NUMBERS (4)

1. Which one of these is a Spice Girl nickname? A) Lairy B) Scary C) Hairy ***(1pt)***

2. Since Nov 2018 how much is the cash prize worth for 3 numbers on the National Lottery? A) £25 B) £20 C) £15 ***(1pt)***

3. What fruit is obtained from a Mirabelle tree? A) Plums B) Cherries C) Pears ***(2pts)***

4. In line of succession to the British throne, what number is Prince Andrew as of March 2020? A) 8th B) 9th C) 10th ***(2pts)***

5. The 1993 Shadowlands is a graphical biographical film centered upon which author? A) JRR Tolkien B) CS Lewis C) A A Milne ***(3pts)***

6. What is the minimum age a person must be to run for the US Presidency? A) 25 B) 30 C) 35 ***(3pts)***

7. Luna Lovegood is a fictional character in which film genre? A) Bond B) Harry Potter C) Carry On ***(4pts)***

8. Boast, Carry and Counterdrop are terms used in: A) Squash B) Badminton C) C) Hurling ***(4pts)***

9. Fray Bentos is a port in which South American country? A) Argentina B) Brazil C) Uruguay ***(5pts)***

10. In the UK Monopoly game, how much is it to buy one station? A) £100 B) £200 C) £300 ***(5pts)***

COMETH THE AXEMEN ANSWERS

1. HE PLAYED IT UPSIDE DOWN
2. T. REX
3. DEEP PURPLE
4. SYD BARRETT
5. 1990
6. HANK B MARVIN
7. C) CREAM
8. ERIC CLAPTON
9. BIG JIM SULLIVAN
10. ALBERT LEE

Answer 6

WORDS & NUMBERS (4) ANSWERS

1. B) SCARY - *1 point*

2. £25 - *1 point*

3. A) PLUMS - *2 points*

4. A) 8th - *2 points*

5. C S LEWIS - *3 points*

6. 35 - *3 points*

7. HARRY POTTER FILM - *4 points*

8. SQUASH - *4 points*

9. URUGUAY - *5 points*

10. £200 - *5 points*

Answer 7

THE LAST SHALL BE FIRST (2)

Last letter of answer to Q1 is 1st letter of Q2 and so on. Last letter of Q10 answer will be 1st letter of Q1

1. Which Bird is the Largest member of the Crow family?

2. In History what name is given to the New Stone Age era?

3. What was the Name of the explorer Jaques Cousteau's ship?

4. By what name is the musical opening of an opera known?

5. What was the first name of U.S President Franklin D. Roosevelts wife?

6. Which Quick, Quick, Slow, Ballroom dance of love and passion originated in Cuba?

7. The Axilla is the medical term for which part of the Human Body?

8. In which Sport would you hear the terms Randi and Rudi?

9. Which Singers songs include – *Let her down easy* and *Fast Love*?

10. Who was the singer who finished 3rd on Fame Academy but went on to have 9 UK hits, 5 of them reaching the top 10 including *If There's Any Justice?*

SOUTH-WEST ENGLAND

1. Originally designed for legions of Cornish miners, meat in one end, sweet in the other, what is the main food symbol of Cornwall?

2. Where is the English Riviera?

3. Which Somerset cathedral city, where the comedic *Hot Fuzz* was filmed, was the smallest city in England in 2011?

4. Gloucester cathedral was used for the filming of scenes in a series of films featuring which spectacled boy wizard?

5. What famous early mediaeval text was found in Exeter, Devon?

6. Which North Devon village has the longest High Street in England?

7. Which explorer sailed from Bristol when he discovered Newfoundland?

8. What is the Cornish word for Cornwall?

9. What author is famously connected to Devon?

10. Located west of the M5 near Bridgwater, the Angel of the South sculpture was better known by which of these names?

THE LAST SHALL BE FIRST (2) ANSWERS

1. RAVEN

Answer 1

2. NEOLITHIC

3. CALYPSO

4. OVERTURE

5. ELEANOR

6. RUMBA

7. ARMPIT

8. TRAMPOLINING

9. GEORGE MICHAEL

10. LEMAR

SOUTH WEST ENGLAND ANSWERS

1. CORNISH PASTY

2. TORBAY *(TORQUAY, BRIXHAM AND PAIGNTON)*

3. WELLS

4. HARRY POTTER

5. THE EXETER BOOK *TREASURY OF ANGLO-SAXON RIDDLES & POETRY*

6. BRAUNTON

7. JOHN CABOT

8. KERNOW

9. DAME AGATHA CHRISTIE

10. THE WILLOW MAN

Answer 9

SHOP 'TIL YOU DROP

Can you identify these shopping centres?

A COUPLE FOR THE KIDDIES!

1. The Wise Old Elf is a character in what TV show?
2. What is the name of Nemo's Dad in Finding Nemo?

SHOP 'TIL YOU DROP ANSWERS

1. CORN EXCHANGE, LEEDS

2. MEADOWHALL,SHEFFIELD

3. EAGLES MEADOW, WREXHAM

4. CRIBBS CAUSEWAY, BRISTOL

5. METRO CENTRE, GATESHEAD

6. BLUEWATER, DARTFORD

7. McARTHUR GLEN, BRIDGEND

8. BRENT CROSS, HENDON

9. CLAYTON SQUARE, LIVERPOOL

10. BULLRING, BIRMINGHAM

A COUPLE FOR THE KIDDIES! ANSWERS

1. BEN AND HOLLY'S LITTLE KINGDOM

2. MARLIN

Co-author Chris, as quizmaster, presents Mike's wife Mo with the winners trophy when her team managed to win one of his popular Quiz Nights at St Mary's, Olveston. Chris presented the quizzes at the church for 8 years.

FIND THE LINK (2)

Answer the questions and find a link

1. In the Holy Communion service which two items represent the body and blood of Jesus Christ?

2. Which 30-second gunfight in Tombstone featuring Wyatt Earp is regarded as the most famous gunfight in American Wild West?

3. Who is the fictional Roman Catholic priest who stars in 51 short stories by GK Chesterton that have also been made into a TV series?

4. What type of dishes link Bombay, Madras, Makhani and Jalfrezi?

5. Which hard rock band had a 1978 hit with *(Don't Fear)The Reaper*?

6. Which German won the Nobel Prize in Physics in 1921?

7. Which traditional English dish is made in 2 layers comprising meat and vegetables topped with mashed potato and cheese and breadcrumbs?

8. What is the other name for calculus, a form of hardened dental plaque?

9. What is the name of an outdoor fast cooking event, most popular in the summer, that has food cooked directly over high heat?

10. Which favourite sweet is most commonly found in dark, milk and white varieties, with cocoa solids contributing to the brown colour?

EXTENDED ROUND (5)
THE BEATLES

An extended round is great to add variety to a quiz night. Sheets are handed out at the beginning of the quiz and answers have to be completed at a later stage of the quiz - quite often the half-time break. Often this takes the form of a Picture Round. But there are other options. This round is a simple job of listing as many nominated hits as you can within a specified time. See the instruction below. The complete list of possible answers is shown on the following page. Good luck.

*Name as many of the Top 20 Hits of **THE BEATLES** as you can in 10 minutes!*

FIND THE LINK (2) ANSWERS

1. BREAD AND WINE
2. GUNFIGHT AT THE OK CORRAL
3. FATHER BROWN
4. CURRY
5. BLUE OYSTER CULT
6. ALBERT EINSTEIN
7. CUMBERLAND PIE
8. TARTAR
9. BARBECUE
10. CHOCOLATE

Answer 3

LINK: SAUCES *(EVEN ALBERT—LOOK IT UP!)*

EXTENDED ROUND (5) ANSWERS
THE BEATLES

A HARD DAY'S NIGHT
ALL YOU NEED IS LOVE
BABY IT'S YOU
BACK IN THE USSR
BALLAD OF JOHN AND YOKO
BEATLES MOVIE MEDLEY
CAN'T BUY ME LOVE
COME TOGETHER
DAY TRIPPER
ELEANOR RIGBY
FREE AS A BIRD
FROM ME TO YOU
GET BACK
HELLO GOODBYE
HELP!
HEY JUDE
I FEEL FINE
I WANT TO HOLD YOUR HAND
LADY MADONNA
LET IT BE
LOVE ME DO
MAGICAL MYSTERY TOUR EP
PAPERBACK WRITER
PENNY LANE
PLEASE PLEASE ME
REAL LOVE
SHE LOVES YOU
SOMETHING
STRAWBERRY FIELDS FOREVER
TICKET TO RIDE
WE CAN WORK IT OUT
YELLOW SUBMARINE
YESTERDAY

WHAT CAR?

Identify the car makes from the logos

QUIRKY!

1. The average person does what thirteen times a day?

2. Who entered a contest to find his own look-alike and came 3rd?

3. What is Scooby Doo's full name?

WHAT CAR? ANSWERS

1. TOYOTA

2. SUBARU

3. LAMBORGHINI

Answer 9

4. BENTLEY

5. FERRARI

6. LEXUS

7. KIA

8. JAGUAR

9. SEAT

10. SKODA

QUIRKY ANSWERS

1. LAUGH
2. CHARLIE CHAPLIN
3. SCOOBERT DOO

For over 25 years I have presented quizzes as part of The Inquizitors team. The other 2 vital members of our team are my wife Mo and son Rob.

FOR THE LOVE OF PETE

1. Who played the part of Lieutenant Columbo in the US TV series for 25 years?

2. Which chemical can be used as a preservative in food and in the manufacture of fireworks?

3. Which footballer holds the record of 125 caps for England?

4. Who became the thirteenth actor to play *Dr Who* on TV?

5. What is the capital of the Channel Island of Guernsey?

6. Who was the author of several novels including *Jaws* and *The Deep*, later adapted into movies?

7. Who was the original lead singer of the band genesis?

8. Which film director / producer's works include *The Lord of the Rings* and *Hobbit* films?

9. Which composer's works include *The Nutcracker* and *Swan Lake*?

10. Which best-selling author is best known for writing crime and thriller novels, and is the creator of Detective Superintendent Roy Grace?

VICIOUS CIRCLE

Last letter of answer to Q1 is the 1st letter of Q2 and so on. Last letter of Q10 answer will be 1st letter of Q1

1. Who played Hawkeye Pearce in the TV series *Mash* ?

2. What was the surname of the Norwegian who reached the South Pole a month before Scott?

3. Who is the Greek goddess of retribution, fate or vengeance?

4. By what name is a narrow stretch of water that connects 2 larger bodies of water or sea known?

5. What word describes either of two parallel latitudes around earth?

6. The characters Billy Bigelow, Julie Jordan and Nettie Fowler are from which musical?

7. Which river gave its name to the battle known as Custer's Last Stand?

8. Which old time comedian's autobiography is titled *Don't Laugh At Me* after one of his hit records?

9. Former Prime Minister Ted Heath owned a series of 5 yachts. What were they named?

10. Name the Native American leader and co-founder of the Iroquois Confederacy, subject of an epic poem by Henry Wadsworth Longfellow.

FOR THE LOVE OF PETE ANSWERS

1. PETER FALK.

2. SALTPETRE

3. PETER SHILTON

4. JODIE WHITTAKER

5. ST PETER PORT

6. PETER BENCHLEY

7. PETER GABRIEL

8. PETER JACKSON

9. PETER TCHAIKOVSKY

10. PETER JAMES

Answer 5

VICIOUS CIRCLE ANSWERS

1. ALAN ALDA

2. AMUNDSEN

3. NEMESIS

4. STRAIT

5. TROPIC

6. CAROUSEL

7. LITTLE BIGHORN

8. NORMAN WISDOM

9. MORNING CLOUD

10. HIAWATHA

Answer 3

OUT OF THEIR COMFORT ZONE

Identify these celebrities, pictured in unusual circumstances

LONDON MARATHON

A few questions about this famous race

1. When was the first London Marathon held?
2. Who ran the fastest women's record time?
3. How many portable toilets are around the course?
4. How many bottles of water are handed out to runners?
5. Who were the first major sponsors of the race?

Inquizitor Rob ran the race in 2017

OUT OF THEIR COMFORT ZONE ANSWERS

1. SIR ALEX FERGUSON
2. ELIZABETH TAYLOR
3. HUGH JACKMAN
4. SHAUN WALLACE
5. GWYNETH PALTROW
6. KEVIN KEEGAN
7. KATHERINE JENKINS
8. DANIEL CRAIG
9. DAME JULIE WALTERS
10. MICHAEL CAINE

Answer 10 - Michael Caine as he usually looked!

LONDON MARATHON ANSWERS

1. 1981
2. PAULA RADCLIFFE IN 2:15:25
3. AROUND 1263 LOOS
4. 650,000 BOTTLES
5. GILLETTE

Chris in action at another successful Quiz Night

TEST YOUR FRIENDS

1. Which artist painted The Water-Lily Pond in 1899?

2. Not scientifically proven but widely held belief that in the human body it takes 17 muscles to smile and 43 minutes to do what?

3. What year was a car with R as the first letter registered in the UK?

4. In Dr Who, what colour is the Doctor's TARDIS—blue, green or red?

5. What colour is a CO2 fire extinguisher?

6. Who is Belfast City Airport named after?

7. Lyrics from which school song? 'The battle's to the strongest, might is always right. Trample on the weakest, glory in their plight'?

8. Which dolls were not bought but 'adopted'?

9. Who wrote the poem that begins 'Tyger! Tyger! Burning bright, in the forests of the night!?

10. Who was the drummer in the Dave Clark Five?

THINK CAREFULLY NOW

1. Blathers, Charlotte and Mr Brownlow are characters from which Charles Dickens tale?

2. Which American actor won the 2002 Oscar for his performance in *Training Day*?
   a) Denzil Washington b) Tom Cruise c) Tom Hanks

3. How many bears lived in the house that Goldilocks went into?

4. What would you commonly use Ethylene Glycol in a car for?

5. Is Bambi the deer a male or female?

6. What does the Scoville Scale measure?

7. Misbehaving students in the first British universities had their names written in black books providing inspiration for which modern day popular phrase?

8. What comes first; lightning or thunder?

9. What is the name of Mr Bean's bear?

10. Which politician served as Mayor of London from 2008 to 2016?

TEST YOUR FRIENDS ANSWERS

1. CLAUDE MONET

2. FROWN

3. 1997

4. BLUE

5. BLACK

6. GEORGE BEST

7. ST TRINIAN'S

8. CABBAGE PATCH

9. WILLIAM BLAKE

10. DAVE CLARK

THINK CAREFULLY NOW ANSWERS

1. OLIVER TWIST
2. A) DENZEL WASHINGTON
3. 3
4. ANTIFREEZE
5. MALE
6. HOTNESS OF CHILLI
7. BLACKLIST
8. LIGHTNING
9. TEDDY
10. BORIS JOHNSON

Answer 5

EXPAND YOUR MIND

1. What was the name of the tiger in The Jungle Book by Rudyard Kipling?

2. If your geographical location is 0 degrees latitude and 0 degrees longitude in which part of the world will you be?

3. What are the streaks of condensed water vapour created iby an airplane or rocket at high altitude?

4. What size of paper measures 210mm x 297mm?

5. Name the German neurologist who discovered the disorder of the brain to cause premature senility?

6. What is the natural colour of caffeine?

7. Which Looney Tunes cartoon character has the scientific name Geococcyx Californianus?

8. What is the flavour of a Pontefract Cake?

9. 'Floreat Etona' is the motto of which British public school?

10. Which hand did Captain Hook lose?

ROUND ROBIN (2)

The last letter of the 1st answer is the first letter of the next answer and so on until Question 10

1. Michael Ebenazer Kwadjo Omari Owuo J is a British rapper, singer and songwriter with a string of hits. What is his stage name?

2. Which English city was called Eboracum by the Romans?

3. What name is used to describe a person who has recurrent inability to resist urges to steal items that you generally don't really need and that usually have little value?

4. In which sport would you have blue and black against red and yellow?

5. Which chemical element has the symbol W?

6. Which extinct early form of man derived its name from a valley in Germany where remains were found in 1856?

7. What novel by William Golding is about a group of boys who struggle for survival stranded on a remote island?

8. Which two word pop song title contains these lyrics: "Where it began, I can't begin to knowing But then I know it's growing strong"

9. What's the surname of 1st woman to fly solo across Atlantic in 1932?

10. What was the name of the 2007 American science fiction action film, which combines computer animation with live-action filming. Directed by Michael Bay, Steven Spielberg as executive producer?

EXPAND YOUR MIND ANSWERS

1. SHERE KHAN

2. ATLANTIC OCEAN

3. CONTRAIL

4. A4

5. ALZHEIMER'S DISEASE

6. WHITE

7. ROAD RUNNER

8. LIQUORICE

9. ETON

10. HIS LEFT HAND

Answer 10

ROUND ROBIN (2) ANSWERS

1. STORMZY

2. YORK

3. KLEPTOMANIAC

4. CROQUET

5. TUNGSTEN

6. NEANDERTHAL

7. LORD OF THE FLIES

8. SWEET CAROLINE (NEIL DIAMOND)

9. EARHART

10. TRANSFORMERS

Answer 6

KNOW-IT-ALL

1. In which home did Catherine Earnshaw live?

2. Which Biblical character gave their name to the world's largest spider?

3. Farmer's daughter Ann Hathaway was said to have married which English playwright?

4. The following sportsmen were World Champions in the1980s. Name their sports:
   A) Norman Dagley B) Egon Muller C) Terry Sullivan

5. Known for *War* singer Charles Hatcher was better known by which name?

6. What was the first burger bar food restaurant in the UK, opened in London in 1954?

7. Which notorious couple lived in 25 Cromwell Street, Gloucester?

8. If you left London on the M4, in which direction would you be travelling?

9. What is the hard tag at the end of a shoelace called?

10. Who plays Agnes Brown in the TV sitcom Mrs Brown's Boys?

CONNECTIONS (6)

Answer questions 1-9 and find a link for answer 10

1. What is the name of the best selling XBOX 360 game that features the character Marcus Fenix?

2. According to Wikipedia, what is the second most popular Romanian TV channel, after ProTV?

3. What is the name of the 1993 track by Pearl Jam that begins with the lyrics: I took a drive today, time to emancipate?

4. What is the name for a ladies bag, most commonly used during the evening, which has no handles and is rectangular in shape?

5. What name is shared by an island in Tasmania, and headwear most commonly worn by women and girls during Easter?

6. What is the name of the punctuation mark, similar to a hyphen but differing primarily in length, and serving different functions?

7. In broadcasting, what term is given to a short break placed between a pause in a program and a commercial break, and vice versa?

8. The Pearl Bridge in Japan, Humber Bridge in the UK, and Golden Gate Bridge in the US are all examples of WHAT type of bridge?

9. What term is given to a summary of any piece of fiction that reveals plot elements which will give away the outcome of a dramatic episode, or the conclusion of the entire work?

10. What's the connection?

KNOW-IT-ALL ANSWERS

1. WUTHERING HEIGHTS

2. GOLIATH

3. WILLIAM SHAKESPEARE

4. A) BILLIARDS B) SPEEDWAY C) BOWLS

5. EDWIN STARR

6. WIMPY BAR

7. FRED & ROSE WEST

8. WEST *(Towards Bristol)*

9. AGLET

10. BRENDAN O'CARROLL

CONNECTIONS (6) ANSWERS

1. GEARS OF WAR

2. ANTENA 1

3. REAR VIEW MIRROR

4. CLUTCH BAG

5. BONNET

6. DASH

7. BUMPER (AS IN BUMPER ADS)

8. SUSPENSION

9. SPOILER

10. ALL PARTS OF A CAR

JUST FOR THE RECORD

Name the album titles

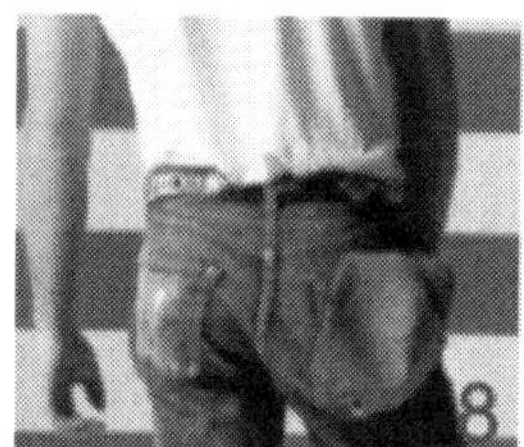

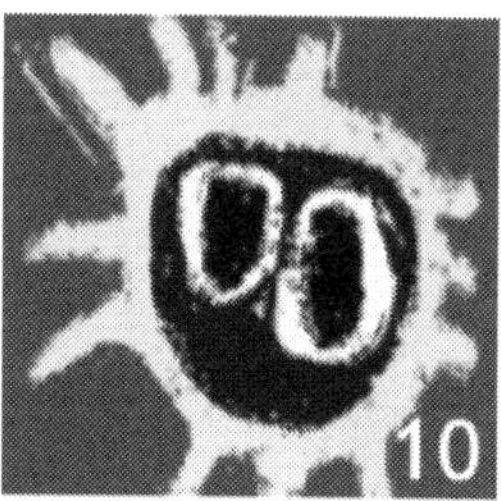

THE VERSATILE SIR DAVID JASON

David played many great roles on TV. What was his character's name in these….

1. Hogfather 2. Ghostboat 3. Porridge 4. Luck Feller 5. Porterhouse Blue 6. All The King's Men 7. Only Fools and Horses 8. Diamond Geezer 9. The Royal Bodyguard 10. Still Open All Hours

And for a bonus: What other role did David play in Only Fools and Horses?

JUST FOR THE RECORD ANSWERS

1. THE BEATLES - REVOLVER

2. BROTHERS IN ARMS - DIRE STRAITS

3. PAUL WELLER - STANLEY ROAD

4. THE EAGLES - HOTEL CALIFORNIA

5. BLUR - MODERN LIFE IS RUBBISH

6. MADONNA - CELEBRATION

7. KATY PERRY - ONE OF THE BOYS

8. BORN IN THE USA - BRUCE SPRINGSTEEN

9. LADY GAG - BORN THIS WAY

10. PRIMAL SCREAM - SCREAMADELICA

THE VERSATILE SIR DAVID JASON ANSWERS

1. ALBERT

2. JACK HARDY

3. BLANCO

4. BERNARD 'SHORTY' MEPSTEAD

5. SKULLION

6. CAPT FRANK BECK

7. DEREK 'DELBOY' TROTTER

8. DES

9. CAPT GUY HUBBLE

10. GRANVILLE

Bonus answer

BONUS: DON VINCENZO OCCHETTI (MIAMI TWICE EPISODE)

NOVELS

1. Which author wrote her only novel *Black Beauty* in the last years of her life when an invalid, dying just 5 months after publication?

2. A) Which dystopian novel features characters Julia, O'Brien & Emmanuel Goldstein? B) Who wrote the book?

3. Which author wrote the Foundation series of science fiction novels?

4. Which prolific crime writer includes *The Big Four*, *Peril At End House* and *Curtain* in their bibliography of 66 detective or mystery novels?

5. A Michael Crichton novel was turned into a 1993 screen blockbuster by Steven Spielberg. What was the title?

6. Ian Fleming is famous for writing the James Bond novels. However he also wrote a story that became a 1968 musical film. Title please.

7. What is the first part of JRR Tolkien's *Lord of the Rings* trilogy called?

8. J, George and Harris form the eponymous title of which book by Jerome K Jerome?

9. Who wrote the classic adventure story about Phileas Fogg and his newly employed French valet's attempt to circumnavigate the world?

10. Who is the main character in John Buchan's *The 39 Steps*?

HAVE A DRINK ON ME

1. What is Homer Simpson's favourite beer?

2. Which Irish company makes Baileys Irish Cream?

3. Cinzano dates to 1757. In which Italian city was the herbal shop that created the 'new' vermouth?

4. Who had a hit in 1961 with *Have A Drink On Me*?

5. With what is the Belgian beer Kriek flavoured?

6. By what name do the British call the light red wines of Bordeaux?

7. Which liqueur is made with whisky and heather honey?

8. If a quality cognac has been in a barrel for 5 and 8 years, how many golden stars would it be awarded?

9. In the French steak dish Tournedos Rossini which fortified wine is used in the making of the demi-glace sauce?

10. From which South American country does Tequila originate?

NOVELS ANSWERS

1. ANNA SEWELL

2. A) 1984 B) GEORGE ORWELL

Answers 2

3. ISAAC ASIMOV

4. DAME AGATHA CHRISTIE

5. JURASSIC PARK

6. CHITTY CHITTY BANG BANG

7. THE FELLOWSHIP OF THE RING

8. THREE MEN IN A BOAT

9. JULES VERNE (AROUND THE WORLD IN 80 DAYS)

10. RICHARD HANNAY

HAVE A DRINK ON ME ANSWERS

1. DUFF

2. GILBEYS

3. TURIN

4. LONNIE DONEGAN

Answer 4

5. CHERRIES

6. CLARET

7. DRAMBUIE

8. 3

9. MADEIRA

10. MEXICO

WATCH THE BIRDIE

Can you identify these garden birds? More difficult in black and white!

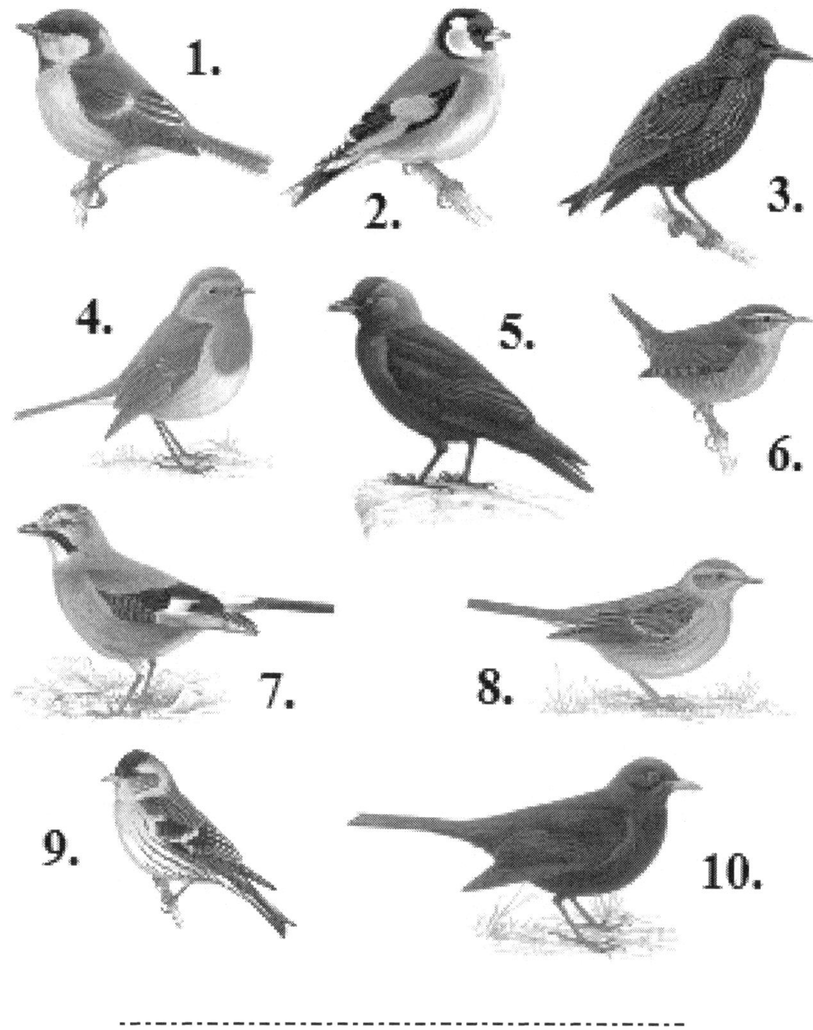

TRIVIAL TITBITS

1. How many hearts does an octopus have?
2. Name the current UK Chancellor of the Exchequer.
3. TORCHWOOD is an anagram of which other TV show?
4. Which colour pill does Neo swallow in The Matrix movie?
5. Ben Stokes inspired England's 2019 Cricket World Cup final victory over New Zealand – who scored the second-highest number of runs in the match for England?

WATCH THE BIRDIE ANSWERS

1. GREAT TIT
2. GOLDFINCH
3. STARLING
4. ROBIN
5. JACKDAW
6. WREN
7. JAY
8. DUNNOCK
9. SISKIN
10. BLACKBIRD

TRIVIAL TITBITS ANSWERS

1. 3
2. RISHI SUNAK
3. DOCTOR WHO
4. RED
5. JOS BUTTLER

SHOWSTOPPERS

Which well-known musicals feature these songs:

1. Bring Him Home

2. Big Spender

3. All That Jazz

4. Love Changes Everything

5. You'll Never Walk Alone

6. I Am What I Am

7. Sit Down You're Rocking The Boat

8. The Greatest Show

9. You Can't Stop The Beat

10. There's No Business Like Showbusiness

CRIME FIGHTERS

Most TV detectives have the support of a willing partner!

1. In the 9th and final series of a popular crime series in 2015, who came out of retirement to once again work alongside DI James Hathaway, portrayed by Laurence Fox?

2. Jason Watkins and Tala Gouveia played mismatched eponymous detectives in which new 2020 series filmed in Bath?

3. Scott & Bailey ran from 2011 until 2016. Who played the two lead characters?

4. DS Havers, played by Sharon Small, was the 8th Earl of Asherton's assistant? What was the name of the series?

5. Captain Harold C Dobey was the boss of which duo of Southern California police detectives?

6. What is the name of Sherlock Holmes' friend and ally?

7. Which TV detective had a dog called simply "Dog"?

8. DI Helen Morton is a leading character in which TV crime series, despite not being featured in the successful Peter Robinson novels?

9. Name the British detective drama TV series set during and shortly after World War II, that was created by Anthony Horowitz?

10. Name the long-running series about a nearly retired employee of the fictional 'Northumberland & City Police', obsessive about her work.

SHOWSTOPPERS ANSWERS

1. LES MISERABLES

2. SWEET CHARITY

3. CHICAGO

4. ASPECTS OF LOVE

5. CAROUSEL

6. LE CAGE AUX FOLLES

7. GUYS AND DOLLS

8. THE GREATEST SHOWMAN

9. HAIRSPRAY

10. ANNIE GET YOUR GUN

CRIME FIGHTERS ANSWERS

1. DI ROBBIE LEWIS

2. McDONALD & DODDS

3. SURANNE JONES and LESLEY SHARP

4. INSPECTOR LINLEY MYSTERIES

5. STARSKY & HUTCH

6. DR JOHN WATSON

7. COLUMBO

8. DCI BANKS

9. FOYLE'S WAR

10. VERA

BLOCKBUSTERS (5)

1. What **A** was the Greek hero who killed the Trojan Hector?

2. What **B** can be a painful swelling on the joint of the big toe?

3. What **C** is the Naval rank held by James Bond?

4. In Heraldry what **D** literally means to the right- hand side?

5. What **E** is the place near Windsor where the Olympic Rowing events were held in 2012?

6. What **F** is wreckage or cargo that stays afloat after a ship sinks?

7. What **G** is a cold Spanish soup made of raw, blended vegetables?

8. What **H** is the surname of the author who wrote *A Farewell To Arms* and *For Whom The Bell Tolls*?

9. Which **I** is the fourth largest island country in the world by population and gained independence from The Netherlands in 1949?

10. Which **J** is the book of the Old Testament between Deuteronomy and Judges?

THE OTHER HALF

1. Who did Jacqueline Bouvier marry in Newport, Rhode in 1953?

2. Which singer's wives have included Ava Gardner and Mia Farrow?

3. Which Flintstone cartoon character is married to Betty?

4. In the year 1472 which future Plantagenet King married Ann Neville?I

5. Baroness Kerren Brady, who stars in The Apprentice and vice-chair of West Ham United is married to a former footballer. Who is he?

6. Fictional character Tracy Di Vicenzo is married in a major film of 1969 before being killed by the main villain. Who was her husband?

7. Who did Clementine Hozier marry in 1905?

8. Which former England rugby union international is married to Zara Phillips. What is his name?

9. In the year 2000 who did actress Catherine Zeta-Jones marry?

10. Who is the other half of the fictional character Ginny Weasly?

BLOCKBUSTERS (5) ANSWERS

1. ACHILLES
2. BUNION
3. COMMANDER
4. DEXTER
5. ETON DORNEY
6. FLOTSAM
7. GAZPACHO
8. HEMINGWAY
9. INDONESIA
10. JOSHUA

Answer 4

THE OTHER HALF ANSWERS

1. JOHN F KENNEDY
2. FRANK SINATRA
3. BARNEY RUBBLE
4. RICHARD III
5. PAUL PESCHISOLIDO
6. JAMES BOND.
7. WINSTON CHURCHILL
8. MIKE TINDALL
9. MICHAEL DOUGLAS.
10. HARRY POTTER

Answer 7

Mike with Ian Holloway, Steve Phillips, Geoff Twentyman and Scott Murray at a 2019 Inquizitors quiz.

EXTENDED ROUND (6)
KYLIE MINOGUE

An extended round is great to add variety to a quiz night. Sheets are handed out at the beginning of the quiz and answers have to be completed at a later stage of the quiz - quite often the half-time break. Often this takes the form of a Picture Round. But there are other options.This round is a simple job of listing as many nominated hits as you can within a specified time. See the instruction below. The complete list of possible answers is shown on the following page. Good luck.

*Name as many of the Top 20 Hits of **KYLIE MINOGUE** as you can in 10 minutes!*

WOMEN'S SPORT

1. Who, in 1977, became the first female jockey to compete in the Grand National?

2. Who won gold medals in the women's featherweight taekwondo class at both the 2012 and 2016 Olympics?

3. Which long-established TV presenter is the only British woman to have won the French Open tennis single title in the Open era?

4. In which event did Charlotte Dujardin win Olympic gold at both the 2012 and 2016 games?

5. Whose husband orchestrated an attack on fellow skater Nancy Kerrigan in 1994?

6. Who captained England's Women to third place at the 2015 FIFA World Cup?

7. Best known for winning four golds at the 1948 Olympics, what was the name of the Dutch athlete nicknamed *The Flying Housewife* ?

8. Who, at 13, was the youngest member of the 2008 GB Paralympic squad but went on to win 2 gold medals?

9. Which female Eventing star was voted BBC Sports Personality of the Year in 1971?

10. Who in 1975 became the first woman to score points at a Formula 1 Grand Prix?

EXTENDED ROUND (6) ANSWERS

KYLIE MINOGUE

ALL THE LOVERS
BETTER THE DEVIL YOU KNOW
BREATHE
CAN'T GET YOU OUT OF MY HEAD
CELEBRATION
CHOCOLATE
COME INTO MY WORLD
CONFIDE IN ME
DID IT AGAIN
ESPECIALLY FOR YOU *(with Jason Donovan)*
FINER FEELINGS
GET OUTTA MY WAY
GIVE ME JUST A LITTLE MORE TIME
GIVING YOU UP
GOT TO BE CERTAIN
HAND ON YOUR HEART
I BELIEVE IN YOU
I SHOULD BE SO LUCKY
IF YOU WERE WITH ME NOW
IN MY ARMS
IN YOUR EYES
INTO THE BLUE
JE NE SAIS PAS POURQUOI
THE LOCO-MOTION
LOVE AT FIRST SIGHT
NEVER TOO LATE
ON A NIGHT LIKE THIS
PLEASE STAY
PUT YOURSELF IN MY PLACE
RED BLOODED WOMAN
SHOCKED
SLOW
SPINNING AROUND
STEP BACK IN TIME
TEARS ON MY PILLOW
2 HEARTS
WHAT DO I HAVE TO DO
WHAT KIND OF FOOL (HEARD IT ALL BEFORE)
WHERE IS THE FEELING
WORD IS OUT
WOULDN'T CHANGE A THING
WOW

WOMEN'S SPORT ANSWERS

1. CHARLOTTE BREW

2. JADE JONES

3. SUE BARKER

4. INDIVIDUAL DRESSAGE

5. TONYA HARDING

6. STEPH HOUGHTON

7. FANNY BLANKERS-KOEN

8. ELLIE SIMMONDS

9. PRINCESS ANNE

10. LELLA LOMBARDI

KNOW YOUR ROAD SIGNS

In the Highway Code, what do these mean?

THE YEAR 2020

1. Which film won Best Picture at the Oscars?
2. What date did the UK go into lockdown?
3. Donald Trump became the third US President to be impeached in February - Who are the two others?
4. Which country legend known for *Ruby* & *Coward of the County* died in March?
5. Which town was Dominic Cummings driving to test his eyesight after being infected with coronavirus?
6. In which US city did George Floyd die after being subdued by police officers?
7. Whose statue was toppled in Bristol in ugly scenes following George Floyd's death in the US?
8. Between February 8 and 9, a powerful storm hit the UK. What was it called?
9. On January 2, why was a third state of emergency declared in New South Wales, Australia?
10. In April, who addressed the nation in their first ever Easter message?

KNOW YOUR ROAD SIGNS? ANSWERS

1. NO VEHICLES CARRYING EXPLOSIVES
2. NO VEHICLES EXCEPT BICYCLES BEING PUSHED
3. T-JUNCTION WITH PRIORITY OVER VEHICLES FROM THE RIGHT
4. SLIPPERY ROAD
5. LONG LOW VEHICLES MAY BE AT RISK OF GROUNDING
6. WILD ANIMALS *(Not just deer)*
7. LEVEL CROSSING WITH BARRIER OR GATE AHEAD
8. OPENING OR SWING BRIDGE
9. VEHICLES MAY PASS EITHER SIDE TO REACH SAME DESTINATION
10. OVERHEAD ELECTRIC CABLE

THE YEAR 2020 ANSWERS

1. PARASITE
2. 23rd MARCH
3. ANDREW JOHNSON & BILL CLINTON
4. KENNY ROGERS

5. BARNARD CASTLE
6. MINNEAPOLIS
7. EDWARD COLSTON
8. STORM CIARA
9. BUSHFIRES
10. THE QUEEN

INQUIZITION

1. Which letters are to the left and right of 'V' on a QWERTY keyboard?

2. Which country planted its flag on the moon for the first time in 2008?

3. In September 2010, former steelworker Philippe Croizon swam the English Channel in just under 14 hours. The record was 6 hrs, 57 mins 50 sec, so why was Croizon's swim so amazing?

4. What might be 12 in London, 10 in New York and 40 in Rome?

5. Which 1959 John Wayne film title is the Mexican name for a river known in the US as 'Rio Grande'?

6. What was the last album recorded by The Beatles?

7. What is London's most frequently stolen street sign?

8. Which river flows into the sea at Plymouth?

9. What is the only landlocked country in South East Asia?

10. What toy was voted the most popular of the 20th century?

WHAT A CLASSIC!

Who composed these well-known pieces of classical music?

1. Rhapsody in Blue

2. Ode to Joy

3. The Hallelujah Chorus

4. The 1812 Overture

5. The Lark Ascending

6. Nessun Dorma

7. Land of Hope and Glory (Pomp and Circumstance)

8. Bolero

9. The Wedding March (in C Major)

10. The Air on a G String

INQUIZITION ANSWERS

1. C AND B

2. INDIA

3. HE WAS A QUADRUPLE AMPUTEE

4. THE SAME DRESS SIZE

5. RIO BRAVO

6. ABBEY ROAD

7. ABBEY ROAD *(yes, same answer as previous question)*

8. PLYM

9. LAOS

10. LEGO

WHAT A CLASSIC! ANSWERS

1. GEORGE GERSHWIN

2. LUDWIG VAN BEETHOVEN

3. GEORGE FRIDERICH HANDEL

4. PYOTR ILYICH TCHAIKOVSKY

5. RALPH VAUGHAN WILLIAMS

6. GIACOMO PUCCINI

7. EDWARD ELGAR

8. MAURICE RAVEL

9. FELIX MENDELSSOHN

10. JOHANN SEBASTIAN BACH

NAME THE GAME

Can you identify these board games?

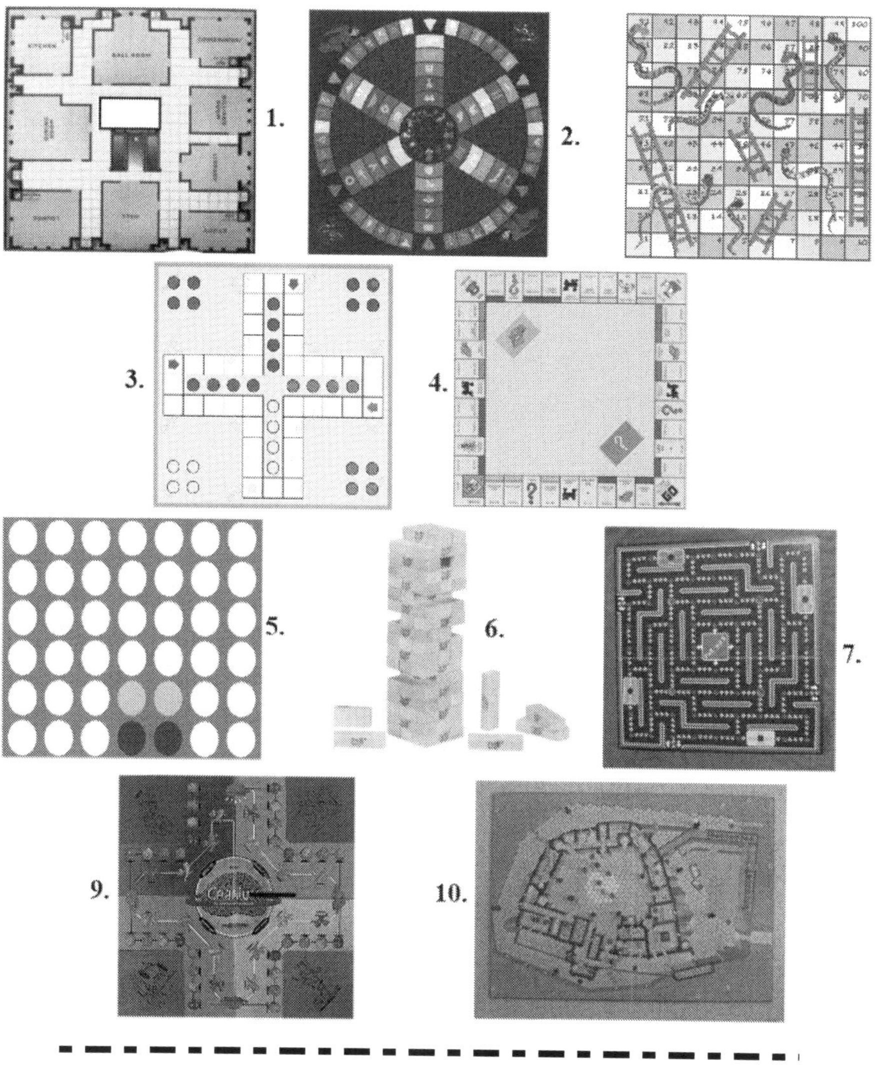

FIVE QUICK QUESTIONS

1. In which year was the popular video game Fortnite first released?

2. Which former US first lady wrote a memoir-turned-Netflix documentary called Becoming?

3. The tallest building in the world is located in which city?

4.What was the name of the tower block where Del Boy and Rodney Trotter lived in Only Fools and Horses?

5. How many horses are on each team in a polo match?

NAME THE GAME ANSWERS

1. CLUEDO

2. TRIVIAL PURSUIT

3. SNAKES AND LADDERS

4. LUDO

5. MONOPOLY

6. CONNECT 4

7. JENGA

8. PAC-MAN

9. CRANIUM

10. ESCAPE FROM COLDITZ

FIVE QUICK QUESTIONS ANSWERS

1. 2017

2. MICHELLE OBAMA

3. DUBAI (BURJ KHALIFA)

4. NELSON MANDELA HOUSE

Whitemead House, Ashton

5. 4

FULL CIRCLE (2)

The last letter of the first answer is the first letter of the next answer and so on until Question 10

1. Which Shakespeare characters final words contain the line Thus with a kiss I die'?

2. Which west coast US state has borders with Washington, Idaho and Nevada?

3. What is the 8th Planet from the Sun?

4. By what name is the sub tropical natural wetlands in Florida known?

5. Which WW 2 battle saw the famed German 6th Army defeated by the Russians in 1943?

6. What type of hat was made famous and worn by Sherlock Holmes?

7. Which 1976 film starred Sylvester Stallone as a boxer?

8. Which Pop song contains these Lyrics. "When I said I needed you, You said you would always stay. It wasn't me who changed but you.."?

9. How many members are in an official tournament Tug of War team?

10. Name the British motoring TV series which took its name from a 1977 programme when launched on BBC2 in October 2002.

WORDS AND NUMBERS (5)

30 POINT ROUND

1. What colour is in the centre of the French National flag? A) Red B) White C) Blue ***(1pt)***
2. Which anniversary did BBC 2 celebrate in 2014?A) 50th B)60th C)70th ***(1pt)***
3. What is the name of the character played by Liza Minnelli in Cabaret?
   A) Sally Bowles B) Sally Fields C) Sally Batts ***(2pts)***

4. March 2020. What is the cost of a UK 2nd class standard letter stamp? A) 63p B) 64p C) 65p ***(2pts)***
5. The Artist George Stubbs is most famous for painting portraits of what?
   A) Ships B) Landscapes C) Horses (3pts)
6. How many imperial Gallons are there in a Firkin? A) 22 B)11 C) 9 ***(3pts)***
7. What is a Dublin Lawyer? A) Irish Solicitor B) A Lobster dish C) Alchoholic drink ***(4pts)***
8. If you had a car with the original Number plate suffix of C in what year was it registered?
   A) 1963 B) 1964 C) 1965 ***(4pts)***
9. In the TV series Star Trek What letters and numbers were on the Starship Enterprise?

   A) NCA 1701 B) NCB 1701 C) NCC 1701 ***(5pts)***
10. Who composed the music for the Musical Carousel
    A) Richard Rogers B) Irving Berlin C) Cole Porter ***(5pts)***

FULL CIRCLE (2) ANSWERS

1. ROMEO
2. OREGON
3. NEPTUNE

4. EVERGLADES
5. STALINGRAD *(STARTED IN AUGUST 1942)*
6. DEERSTALKER
7. ROCKY
8. YOU DON'T HAVE TO SAY YOU LOVE ME *(DUSTY SPRINGFIELD)*
9. EIGHT
10. TOP GEAR

WORDS AND NUMBERS (5) ANSWERS

1. B) WHITE - *1 point*

2. A) 50th - 1 point

3. A) SALLY BOWLES - *2 points*

4. C) 65p - *2 points*

5. C) HORSES - *3 points*

6. C) 9 - *3 points*

7. B) A LOBSTER DISH - *4 points*

8) C) 1965 - *4 points*

9. C) NCC 1701 - *5 points*

10. A) RICHARD RODGERS - *5 points*

EXTENDED ROUND (7)
MARIAH CAREY

An extended round is great to add variety to a quiz night. Sheets are handed out at the beginning of the quiz and answers have to be completed at a later stage Of the quiz - quite often the half-time break. Often this takes the form of a Picture Round. But there are other options. This round is a simple job of listing as many nominated hits as you can within a specified time. See the instruction below. The complete list of possible answers is shown on the following page. Good luck.

Name as many of the Top 20 Hits of
MARIAH CAREY as you can in 10 minutes!

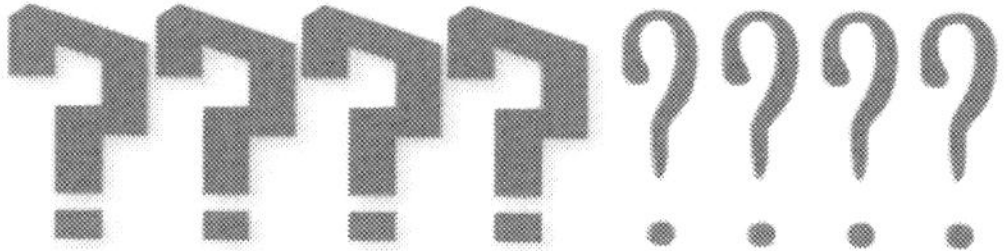

MEMORABLE FIRST LINES

Name the song from the opening lines

1. "I need to be myself / I can't be no one else / I'm feeling supersonic / Give me gin and tonic. / You can have it all but how much do you want..

2. "We'll be fighting in the streets / With our children at our feet."

3. "She came from Greece. She had a thirst for knowledge. / She studied sculpture at Saint Martin's College."

4. "It's a god-awful small affair / To the girl with the mousy hair."

5. "Once upon a time you dressed so fine / Threw the bums a dime in your prime, didn't you?"

6. "In France a skinny man died of a big disease with a little name."

7. "I am a lineman for the county / And I drive the main road / Searchin' in the sun for another overload."

8. "You were working as a waitress in a cocktail bar."

9. "A candy-coloured clown they call the sandman / Tiptoes to my room every night."

10. "I may not always love you / But as long as there are stars above you / you never need to doubt it..."

EXTENDED ROUND (7) ANSWERS
MARIAH CAREY

AGAINST ALL ODDS
ALL I WANT FOR CHRISTMAS IS YOU
ALWAYS BE MY BABY
ANYTIME YOU NEED A FRIEND
BOY (I NEED YOU)
CAN'T LET GO
DON'T FORGET ABOUT US
DREAMLOVER
EMOTIONS
FANTASY
GET YOUR NUMBER
HEARTBREAKER
HERO
HONEY
I STILL BELIEVE
I WANT TO KNOW WHAT LOVE IS
I'LL BE THERE
IT'S LIKE THAT
LOVERBOY
MAKE IT HAPPEN
MY ALL
ONE SWEET DAY
OPEN ARMS
SHAKE IT OFF
THANK GOD I FOUND YOU
THROUGH THE RAIN
TOUCH MY BODY
VISION OF LOVE
WE BELONG TOGETHER
WHEN YOU BELIEVE
WITHOUT YOU

MEMORABLE FIRST LINES ANSWERS

1. SUPERSONIC - OASIS
2. WON'T GET FOOLED AGAIN - THE WHO
3. COMMON PEOPLE - PULP
4. LIFE ON MARS - DAVID BOWIE
5. LIKE A ROLLING STONE - BOB DYLAN
6. SIGN O' THE TIMES - PRINCE
7. WICHITA LINEMAN - GLEN CAMPBELL
8. DON'T YOU WANT ME - HUMAN LEAGUE
9. IN DREAMS - ROY ORBISON
10. GOD ONLY KNOWS - BEACH BOYS

Answer 4

BLOCKBUSTERS (6)

1. What **S** is the indigenous faith of the Japanese people?

2. What **EBB** was a female Victorian poet born in 1806, died 1861 in Florence?

3. What **DLTSGDOM** was a hit for Elton John and George Michael?

4. **CB** are the initials of which doctor who performed the first human heart transplant in 1967?

5. Which **BB** composer wrote the operas Billy Budd and Peter Grimes?

6. Which **BM** was commander of the British 8th Army in the desert in WWII?

7. What **DNFMOMD** is the theme to the 1952 cowboy film High Noon?

8. Which **SM** was elected as Australian Prime Minister in 2018?

9. The Titanic was titled RMS Titanic. What does the **RMS** stand for?

10. **GC**, **JC**, **BM**, and **RW** were the famous back four of England's 1966 World Cup winning team – *(1 pt for each one named).*

CONNECTIONS (7)

Answer the 10 questions and then use your answers to find a link

1. What was destroyed by fire in Hong Kong harbour in 1972, during major restorations?
2. In the 1970s, which brand of beer was said to 'work wonders'?
3. What was the name of the character played by Humphrey Bogart in the 1941 film adaptation of Dashiell Hammett's *The Maltese Falcon*?
4. Whose daughters were called Regan, Goneril and Cordelia?
5. What is the name of the British comedy actor famed for his roles as Owen in *The Vicar of Dibley* and Colin Ball in *Only Fools and Horses?*
6. Sam Neill played the title role in which 1983 TV drama series?
7. Which American author wrote the novels *White Fang* and *The Call of the Wild*?
8. Which 1990 No 1 hit for the Steve Miller Band had been used in a Levi Jeans commercial?
9. The film *Apocalypse Now* was based on which Joseph Conrad novel?
10. Which 1963 R&B song, written by duo Bob and Earl, has been covered by Booker T and the MGs and, in 1986, the Rolling Stones?

And the connection between the answers?

BLOCKBUSTERS (6) ANSWERS

1. SHINTO
2. ELIZABETH BARRETT BROWNING
3. DON'T LET THE SUN GO DOWN ON ME
4. CHRISTIAN BARNARD

5. BENJAMIN BRITTEN
6. BERNARD MONTGOMERY
7. DO NOT FORSAKE ME O MY DARLING
8. SCOTT MORRISON
9. ROYAL MAIL STEAMER
10. GEORGE COHEN, JACK CHARLTON, BOBBY MOORE, RAY WILSON

CONNECTIONS (7) ANSWERS

1. RMS QUEEN ELIZABETH
2. DOUBLE DIAMOND
3. SAM SPADE
4. KING LEAR
5. ROGER LLOYD PACK

6. REILLY, ACE OF SPIES
7. JACK LONDON
8. THE JOKER
9. HEART OF DARKNESS
10. HARLEM SHUFFLE

CONNECTION: PLAYING CARDS

LUCKY DIP

1. What would Napoleon have found it almost impossible to do tonight, or any other night, in bed?

2. Who ate poisoned cakes, was shot twice, but only died after being tied up and thrown in a river?

3. Where did Chilli Con Carne originate?

4. What is the fastest bird in the world?

5. Which English premiership team began life as Dial Square FC?

6. How many different United Kingdom Prime Ministers have there been in Queen Elizabeth's reign?

7. How many hands does Big Ben have?

8. What is a cock-up splint used to support?

9. Approximately how many lumps of sugar are used in a can of non-diet fizzy drink?

10. What was the name of Noddy's house?

KNOWLEDGE QUEST

1. Which common phrase probably originated from the Window tax levied by King George III?

2. What does a gymnophobe fear?

3. The suspicions of his last victim's daughter and a taxi driver fast losing elderly customers led to the arrest of which mass murderer in 1998?

4. How many noughts are there in the written number ten million?

5. Two well-known TV programmes introduced by David Attenborough, *United* and *Divided* were about which endearing animals?

6. What was the occupation of the person whose spouse was responsible for amputating the rear appendages of a trio of visually challenged rodents?

7. Zagreb is the capital of which Balkan country?

8. Approximately how often is an earthquake detected in the UK?

9. What became fully available again on 5th February 1953, having been rationed since 1940?

10. What is an addax: A) antelope B) snake C) notched reverse blade axe D) counting frame?

LUCKY DIP ANSWERS

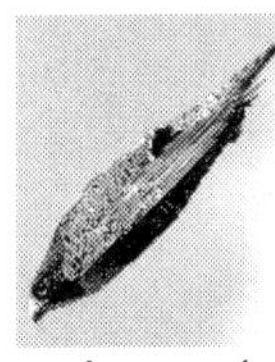
Answer 4

1. SLEEP *(he suffered from insomnia)*

2. RASPUTIN

3. TEXAS

4. PEREGRINE FALCON *(112 mph)*

5. ARSENAL

6. 14 *(Churchill, Eden, MacMillan, Douglas-Home, Wilson (twice), Heath, Callaghan Thatcher, Major, Blair, Brown, Cameron, May, Johnson)*

7. NONE— IT'S A BELL

8. ELBOW

9. 10

10. HOUSE FOR ONE

KNOWLEDGE QUEST ANSWERS

1. DAYLIGHT ROBBERY

2. NUDITY

3. DR HAROLD SHIPMAN

4. 7 *(10,000,000)*

5. MEERKATS

6. FARMER *(THREE BLIND MICE)*

7. CROATIA

8. EVERY 4 DAYS

9. SWEETS

10. A) AN ANTELOPE

WORLD OF KNOWLEDGE

1. The city of Granada is separated from the Mediterranean by which mountain range?

2. Wilson's Disease affects which part of the body: A) the lungs B) the bone marrow C) the nervous system and the liver D) the heart?

3. Which Scottish football team were previously known as Ferranti Thistle and Meadowbank Thistle?

4. In the crab family what is unique about the robber crab?

5. Which civilisation invented concrete?

6. True or false? Texas is America's largest state.

7. Which TV presenter, actor, comedian and writer was jailed, aged 17, for credit card fraud?

8. In June 1999 who became the first England player to be sent off in a football international match at Wembley?

9. On The Beatles Abbey Road album cover, whom is last in line on the zebra crossing?

10. In what kind of building did multinational company Hewlett-Packard first start as a business in 1939?

THIS AND THAT (2)

1. Which US state has towns named Oatmeal, Gun Barrel City, Happy and Uncertain?

2. A Baker's Dozen plus a trio plus a gross gives a total which when divided by a score =?

3. If you were invited to a party what does BYOB mean?

4. Flowing into the North Sea below Dundee, what is the longest river located entirely within Scotland?

5. In the proverb what do 'only fools and horses' do?

6. Where is Anne, Princess Royal currently in the order of succession to the British throne?

7. In which English county would you find the small village Blubberhouses?

8. Which famous seaman, son of a Norfolk clergyman, joined the navy at the age of 12 and died in 1805, having risen to the highest naval rank?

9. How many inches are there in a mile?

10. How many dots appear on a standard 28-piece set of dominoes?

WORLD OF KNOWLEDGE ANSWERS

1. SIERRA NEVADA

2. C) THE NERVOUS SYSTEM AND THE LIVER

3. LIVINGSTON

4. IT CAN CLIMB TREES

5. THE ROMANS

6. TRUE

7. STEPHEN FRY

8. PAUL SCHOLES

9. GEORGE HARRISON

10. A GARAGE

THIS AND THAT (2) ANSWERS

1. TEXAS

2. 8 (13 + 3 + 144 ÷ 20 =)

3. BRING YOUR OWN BOTTLE

4. RIVER TAY

5. WORK

6. ELEVENTH

7. NORTH YORKSHIRE

8. LORD HORATIO NELSON

9. 63,360

10. 168

PANDORA'S BOX

1. Which Indian city was renamed Chennai in 1996?

2. Which name is shared by a dwarf planet and the ruler of the underworld in classical mythology?

3. Which year? Fred & Rosemary West arrested for murders; Ayrton Senna killed in Grand Prix crash; Britain's national Lottery gets under way; car Ferry Estonia sinks in the Baltic.

4. Who was the Artistic Director of Isles of Wonder, the opening ceremony of the 2012 London Summer Olympic Games?

5. How many balls of marzipan are traditionally placed around the top of a Simnel Cake at Easter?

6. What type of doctor was Doc Holliday, famed for the OK Corral Gunfight?

7. The World Health Organisation is based in which city? a) London b) Geneva c) Cologne

8. Stirling Castle and Borthwick Castle are both reputed to be haunted by the ghost of which historical figure?

9. In 565 AD St Columba is said to have seen which creature of legend?

10. Which smart bird always got the better of Wile E Coyote?

IT HAPPENED IN FEBRUARY

1. Manchester United players and 15 other passengers were killed in February 1958 in an accident that became known as what?

2. In what year did women over 30, provided they met certain qualifications, get the right to vote in the UK? a) 1918 b) 1924 c) 1928

3. Which landscape architect, who died in February 1783, is dubbed 'England's Greatest Gardener' whose work can be seen at many great estates including Blenheim Palace and Harewood House?

4. In which unusual location was Elizabeth when she succeeded to the UK throne on the death of her father ?

5. Waitangi Day, celebrated on the 6th Feb, commemorates the signing of the treaty which is regarded as the founding of which island country?

6. In 1587 which queen was executed for her part in the 'Babington Plot' to murder her cousin?

7. In February 2013 which US State became the last to certify Amendment Thirteen of the US Constitution and thus became the final state to abolish slavery?

8. Henry E Steinway who died in Feb 1871 was a German American businessman who founded a company making what?

9. What date is mostly celebrated by people who are in love, including couples that are married or just dating?

10. What is the birthstone for February?

PANDORA'S BOX ANSWERS

1. MADRAS

2. PLUTO

3. 1994

4. DANNY BOYLE

5. 11 *(each disciple less Judas)*

6. DENTISTRY

7. B) GENEVA

8. MARY, QUEEN OF SCOTS

9. LOCH NESS MONSTER

10. ROAD RUNNER

IT HAPPENED IN FEBRUARY ANSWERS

1. MUNICH AIR DISASTER

2. A) 1918

3. LANCELOT 'CAPABILITY' BROWN

4. IN A TREE HOUSE AT THE TREETOPS HOTEL IN KENYA

5. NEW ZEALAND

6. MARY, QUEEN OF SCOTS

7. MISSISSIPPI

8. PIANOS

9. FEBRUARY 14TH *(VALENTINES DAY)*

10. AMETHYST

ONE THING AND ANOTHER

1. What is a larnax?

2. Name the only footballer to have scored goals in the Manchester, Liverpool and Glasgow derby matches?

3. From which country did French Fries originate?

4. What could be a broomstick, ballerina or a poodle?

5. What is the world's most popular non-alcoholic drink?

6. What is the most popular fruit in the world?

7. Which is the only team in the 92 top football teams in England whose name begins with 5 consecutive consonants?

8. In golf, what is a condor or vulture?

9. Which classical ballet tells the story of a girl who visits the Land of Sweets on Christmas Eve?

10. Which animal is listed first in the Oxford English Dictionary?

TRAVELLERS

1. Whose 1497 discovery of the coast of North America under commission of Henry VII of England is the earliest known European exploration of coastal North America since Norse visits to Finland in the 11th century? He has a tower named after him in Bristol, UK.

2. Who was the first woman to fly solo across the Pacific Ocean?

3. Which two men were the first to summit Mount Everest in 1953?

4. Who is best known for speed-summiting six of the world's tallest peaks, including Everest, in just one month in 2019?

5. Dr Robert Ballard, oceanographer and marine biologist with Woods Hole Oceanographic Institution, found the remains of what in 1985?

6. Which Victorian explorer was the first European to see and name the Victoria Falls on the Zambezi river?

7. What nationality was Sir Henry Morton Stanley, the journalist and explorer, famous for his exploration of central Africa and his search for missionary and explorer David Livingstone?

8. How many people have set foot on the moon?

9. Which European explorer discovered and named Lake Victoria while searching for the source of the Nile river?

10. The 16th century Spanish explorer Juan Ponce de Leon allegedly searched for what mythical wonder in Florida?

ONE THING AND ANOTHER ANSWERS

1. COFFIN MADE OF TERRACOTTA
2. ANDREI KANCHELSKIS
3. BELGIUM
4. A SKIRT
5. COFFEE

7. CRYSTAL PALACE
8. A SCORE OF 4 SHOTS UNDER PAR FOR A HOLE
9. THE NUTCRACKER
10. AARDVARK

TRAVELLERS ANSWERS

1. JOHN CABOT *(GIOVANNI CABOTO)*
2. BETTY MILLER *(1963)*
3. TENZING NORGAY AND EDMUND HILLARY
4. NIRMAL 'NIMS' PURJA
5. RMS TITANIC
6. DAVID LIVINGSTONE
7. WELSH

9. JOHN HANNING SPEKE
10. FOUNTAIN OF YOUTH

GET IT RIGHT

1. Who was hanged in 1829 for grave robbing after his partner gave evidence against him?

2. If you have a double X chromosome are you male or female?

3. Which country won the Eurovision Song Content three years in succession from1992 and 1994?

4. What is the major tourist attraction in the Texas town of San Antonio?

5. What is the name of the two-coloured oblong cake usually covered in almond paste?

6. What type of 'ologist' was Quasimodo?

7. By what name is the 15th July known?

8. Name three countries of Europe that have names that begin and end with the letter 'A' (in English)

9. Identify the famous Britain explorer beheaded in the Tower of London in 1618.

10. Following a long running dispute with Greece, the Republic of Macedonia renamed itself as....?

GENERAL KNOWLEDGE

1. What is the highest peak in Scotland after Ben Nevis?

2. What did Wonder Woman's lasso always make people do?

3. What links Hampstead Heath, Reigate Priory and Maidenhead?

4. Which London Underground line serves Heathrow Airport?

5. Which country has as its anthem, *The Soldier's Song*?

6. From what did God create Adam?

7. Why did the old lady who swallowed a fly, later swallow a bird ?

8. Multiply a soccer team by the cardinal points on a compass, double the figure and divide by 11?

9. Which invention was first usefully applied to a packet of chewing gum in 1974?

10. What type of transport was invented by Gottleib Daimler?

GET IT RIGHT ANSWERS

1. WILLIAM BURKE
2. FEMALE (MALE X/Y)
3. IRELAND
4. THE ALAMO
5. BATTENBURG
6. A CAMPANOLOGIST *(Bellringer)*
7. WILLIAM BURKE
8. FEMALE (MALE X/Y)
9. IRELAND
10. THE ALAMO

Answer 6

GENERAL KNOWLEDGE ANSWERS

1. BEN MACDUI
2. TELL THE TRUTH
3. ALL WERE ORIGINAL FA CUP ENTRANTS
4. PICCADILLY LINE
5. IRELAND
6. DUST
7. TO CATCH THE SPIDER
8. 8
9. A BAR-CODE
10. A MOTORCYCLE

Answer 2

MIXED BAG (2)

1. Alfred Wainwright was the originator of what hike covering the Lake District, Yorkshire Dales and the North York Moors?

2. In April 2019 a major fire broke out in which iconic building in France?

3. The 2019 Cricket World Cup was won by which country?

4. Which small Arctic whale has a long, straight tusk originating from its teeth?

5. Which UK tourist attraction is on the site of an 8thC fortress?

6. Which famous London police station closed in 1992 after 230 years?

7. What is the flavour of a Devil's Food Cake?

8. In which country was the composer Gustav Holst born?

9. Which leader of the Apache tribe died in 1909?

10. Where are the Union Hills and Onchan Head in the British Isles?

CORNUCOPIA

1. The Oresund Bridge connects Denmark with which neighbouring country?
2. Who was the alter ego—Dr Jekyll or Mr Hyde?
3. Edward I, father of 18 legitimate children, was called Longshanks due to the length of his what?
4. Aspirin was first synthesized from the bark of which riverbank tree?
5. The passengers of the Titanic waved goodbye to which British port?
6. London is the UK's most popular tourist destination. Which City comes second?
7. Trachoma is a contagious disease affecting which body part?
8. Which is the oldest of these chocolate bars: Fry's Turkish Delight; Cadbury's Dairy Milk or Fry's Chocolate Cream?

9. Which famous statesman was born in a ladies' room during a dance?

10. Two groups had the most UK No.1 hits during the Nineties with 8 each, one was Take That, but which was the other group?

MIXED BAG (2) ANSWERS

1. COAST TO COAST WALK (196 miles St Bees-Robin Hood's Bay)

2. NOTRE DAME

3. ENGLAND

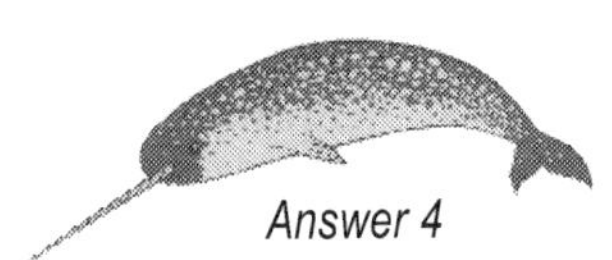

Answer 4

4. NARWHAL

5. ALTON TOWERS

6. BOW STREET

7. CHOCOLATE

8. ENGLAND

9. GERONIMO

10. ISLE OF MAN

CORNUCOPIA ANSWERS

1. SWEDEN

2. MR HYDE

3. LEGS

4. WILLOW

5. SOUTHAMPTON

6. EDINBURGH

7. THE EYE

8. FRY'S CHOCOLATE CREAM

9. SIR WINSTON CHURCHILL

10. THE SPICE GIRLS

Answer 3

FIND THE LINK (3)

Find the connection between all the correct answers FOR A 5 POINT BONUS

1. What colour flag orders a driver to return to the pits in motor racing?

2. 'Rub-a-dub-dub, three men in a tub, the butcher, the baker and whom?

3. Name the famous concert hall in London. A treasured and distinctive building, it can seat 5,272.

4. What bird in some countries is also a symbol of pride or vanity, due to the way the bird struts and shows off its plumage?

5. What Beatles album originally included Eleanor Rigby, Yellow Submarine and Taxman?

6. Name the main research library of Oxford University — one of the oldest libraries in Europe, ?

7. Name the American singer, songwriter, rapper, producer, and actor who was in Goodie Mob and later was part of the soul duo Gnarls Barkley.

8. Nigel Slater, Lorraine Pascale and Madhur Jaffrey all appear on TV programmes centered upon which place of work?

9. Who became the world's highest paid actress in 2018 having starred in films like Black Widow, Iron Man 2 The Jungle Book (2016) as a voice)?

10. Name the comparatively soft, malleable bluish grey metal used for flushing on roofs.

What links the answers?

LUCKY DIP (2)

1. Who was chuffed at pulling Annie and Clarabel?
2. How was Indira Gandhi related to Mahatma Gandhi?
3. What is London's oldest football club?
4. Before adopting the Euro, what was the unit of currency of Greece?
5. Which TV series featured mice on the 'Mouse Organ'?
6. Paul Thomson, Bob Hardy, Alex Kapranos and Nick McCarthy comprised which band?
7. In which city other than London would you find Kings Cross, Paddington, Oxford Street and Hyde Park?
8. Add the year of the Battle of Hastings to that of the D-Day landings?
9. What is the name of the metal web that divides the dartboard into sections?
10. Which salad's ingredients include walnuts, celery and apples gets its name from a New York hotel?

FIND THE LINK (3) ANSWERS

1. BLACK

2. THE CANDLESTICK MAKER

3. THE ROYAL ALBERT HALL

Answer 3

4. PEACOCK

5. REVOLVER

6. BODLEIAN LIBRARY

7. CEE LO GREEN

8. THE KITCHEN

9. SCARLETT JOHANSSON

10. LEAD

LUCKY DIP (2) ANSWERS

1. THOMAS THE TANK ENGINE

2. SHE WAS NOT RELATED

3. FULHAM *(1879)*

4. DRACHMA

5. BAGPUSS

6. FRANZ FERDINAND

7. SYDNEY

Answer 7

8. 3010 (1066 + 1944)

9. SPIDER

10. WALDORF SALAD

WORDS AND NUMBERS (6)

30 point round

1. Which Political party won 3.8 million votes in the 2015 election, but only 1 seat in Parliament?
   A) Liberal Democrats B) Green PartyC) UKIP ***(1pt)***

2. How many points is W worth in Scrabble? A) 2 B) 3 C) 4 ***(1pt)***

3. What colour is the Circle line on the London Underground map? A) Red B) Yellow C) Blue ***(2pts)***

4. In the rhyme *Sing A Song of Sixpence*, how many blackbirds are baked in a pie?
   A) 4 and 10 B) 4 and 20 C) 4 and 30 ***(2pts)***

5. Who was the US president in 1945 at the time of the German surrender in Europe?
   A) Roosevelt B) Eisenhower C) Truman ***(3pts)***

6. In the UK a Crystal wedding anniversary celebrates how many years of marriage?
   A) 14 B) 15 C) 20 ***(3pts)***

7. Which Bronte sister wrote *The Tenant of Wildfell Hall*? A) Anne B) Emily C) Charlotte ***(4pts)***

8. How UK many fluid ounces in a Pint? A)18 B) 20 C) 22 ***(4pts)***

9. After he retired what activity was pursued by legendary fictional detective Sherlock Holmes?
   A) Bird Watching B) Wine Making C) Bee Keeping ***(5pts)***

10. In which Year was the SS Great Britain brought back to Bristol from the Falklands?
    A) 1970 B) 1973 C) 1975 ***(5pts)***

DOUBLE CONNECTION

Find a link between the 2 descriptions used for each question. Then find a 2nd link between the 9 answers!

1. Murder victim in Cluedo : Son of Edward III

2. Frank Sinatra nickname : Elvis' Suede Shoes

3. McPhee : Mrs Baylock in The Omen

4. A bird of the Corvus genus : The song 'If It Makes You Happy'

5. 18th century British Prime Minister : Tree used to make cordial or gin

6. A small pipe used for drinking : Dry stalks of cereal plants

7. Ursula Andress role in Dr No : Bobby Goldsboro 1968 hit

8. A species of Waterfowl : A difficult ceremonial marching style

9. Double Eurovision winner : Xmen Wolverine alias

10. What is the connection between the 9 answers

WORDS AND NUMBERS (6) ANSWERS

1. C) UKIP

2. C) 4

3. B) YELLOW

4. B) 4 AND 20

5. C TRUMAN

6. B) 15

7. A) ANNE

8. B) 20

9. C) BEEKEEPING

10. A) 1970

Answer 7

DOUBLE CONNECTION ANSWERS

Answer 1

1. BLACK (Dr Black and Edward the Black Prince)

2. BLUE (Ol Blue Eyes and Blue Suede Shoes)

. NANNY (Nanny McPhee and Nanny in The Omen)

4. CROW (Crow and Sheryl Crow)

;. ELDER (William Pitt the Elder and the Elder tree)

6. STRAW (A drinking straw and Straw)

7. HONEY (Honey Rider and Honey

8. GOOSE (Goose and Goose-step)

9. LOGAN (Johnny Logan and Logan)

10. TYPES OF BERRIES

(Blackberry, Blueberry, Nannyberry, Crowberry, Elderberry, Strawberry, Honeyberry, Gooseberry, Loganberry)

UK SIT-COMS

Can you name these familiar comedy shows?

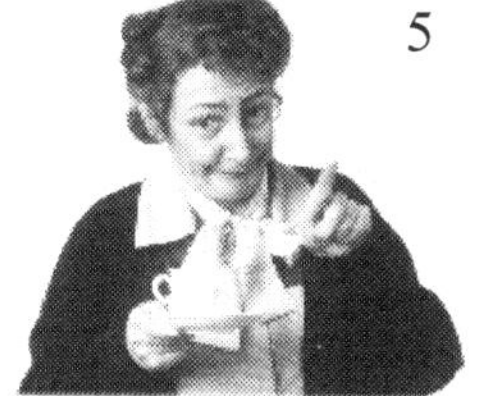

CALL MY BLUFF

What is the correct description of these rare words

1. **FRIABLE** - A) EDIBLE B) CRUMBLY C) CAPABLE OF BEING PRONOUNCED
2. **BARYON** - A) TIP OF A TREE ROOT B) CHEMICAL ELEMENT C) ELEMENTARY PARTICLE
3. **QINDAR** - A) AFRICAN PYGMY DEER B) ALBANIA CURRENCY C) RADIOACTIVE PARTICLE
4. **KOKAKO** - JAPANESE WIND INSTRUMENT B) NEW ZEALAND CROW C) HAWAIIAN PARROT
5. **NIPA** - A) JUMPING FLEA B) SOUTH AMERICAN FRUIT C) PINE TREE

UK SIT-COMS ANSWERS

1. DINNERLADIES

2. FAWLTY TOWERS

3. LAST OF THE SUMMER WINE

4. KATE & KOJI

5. FATHER TED

6. ONLY FOOLS AND HORSES

7. ALL ROUND TO MRS BROWN'S

8. PETER KAY'S CAR SHARE

9. BREEDERS

10. THE ROYLE FAMILY

CALL MY BLUFF ANSWERS

1. B) CRUMBLY

2. C) ELEMENTARY PARTICLE

3. B) ALBANIAN CURRENCY

4. B) NEW ZEALAND CROW

5. C) PINE TREE

Mike in quizmaster mode!

STRINGALONGS

The answer to each question contains a word repeated in the next correct answer

1. Who was the leader of the Peasants Revolt against King Richard II in 1381?

2. Which English football commentator has worked as a commentator for Sky Sports since 1990?

3. In August 1999 a farmer from Norfolk, England, who shot a burglar dead in his home was controversially convicted of murder. What was his name?

4. The son of a former chairman of Durham Conservative Association became Labour leader and subsequently prime minister in 1997. Who is he?

5. What is the title of the supernatural horror film about three student filmmakers who hike in the Black Hills near Burkittsville, Maryland in 1994 to film a documentary?

6. Peter, Susan, Lucy and Edmund are the four main characters in which fantasy novel by CS Lewis?

7. Name the animated musical drama film produced by Walt Disney, with songs by Tim Rice and Elton John, which won two Golden Globes?

8. Who was the American Christian minister and activist who became the most visible spokesperson and leader in the Civil Rights Movement from 1955 until his assassination in 1968?

9. The legend of which 'Great' king is about some burnt cakes?

10. Name the English film director and producer who is known as *The Master of Suspense*, who directed over 50 feature films including *Psycho* and *Rear Window*.

CRIME AND PUNISHMENT

1. What was the name given to Donald Nielson who in 1976 was given 5 life sentences?

2. In 1955 who was the last woman to be hanged in Britain?

3. In which road in Gloucester did Fred and Rose West live?

4. On which ship was Dr Crippen the first suspect captured with the aid of wireless telegraphy?

5. Which forensic technique was developed by Sir Alec Jeffreys at Leicester University?

6. Which osteopath was at the centre of the Profumo affair?

7. What Epsom Derby winner, an IRA kidnap victim in 1983 was never seen again?

8. What weapon was used to kill Bulgarian defector Georgi Markov in London in 1978?

9. How did Anne Bonney become notorious in the 18th Century?

10. Which criminal was released by Pontius Pilate instead of Jesus?

STRINGALONGS ANSWERS

Answer 1

1. WAT TYLER
2. MARTIN TYLER
3. TONY MARTIN
4. TONY BLAIR
5. THE BLAIR WITCH PROJECT
6. THE LION, THE WITCH AND THE WARDROBE
7. THE LION KING
8. MARTIN LUTHER KING JR
9. KING ALFRED
10. ALFRED HITCHCOCK

CRIME AND PUNISHMENT ANSWERS

1. THE BLACK PANTHER
2. RUTH ELLIS
3. CROMWELL STREET
4. SS MONTROSE
5. DNA FINGERPRINTING AND PROFILING
6. STEPHEN WARD

8. AN UMBRELLA (FIRED RICIN INJECTED PELLET)
9. SHE WAS A PIRATE
10. BARABBAS

WHODUNNIT QUEEN

All about Agatha Christie

1. In which town in Devon was Agatha Christie born in 1890?

2. What was Miss Marple's first name?

3. Which play, written by Christie, opened in 1952 and is still running?

4. Agatha's first novel, The Mysterious Affair at Styles introduced which detective?

5. In 1957 Agatha Christie became the president of which Club?

6. The Agatha Christie Mile in Devon has how many points of interest?

7. Agatha Christie is buried at St. Mary's Churchyard in Cholsey. Which county is Cholsey in?

8. What was Agatha Christie's occupation during World War I?

9. Miss Marple lives in which village?

10. Who played Poirot in the 1974 film version of Murder on the Orient Express?

CONTINUITY

The answer to each question contains a word repeated in the answer to the next question

1. What was moved from England to Lake Havasu City in Arizona in 1968?

2. Which 1981 horror film tells of two American students who are attacked by a werewolf while on a backpacking holiday in England?

3. In which movie did Kevin Spacey play advertising executive Lester Burnham?

4. Which equine literary character shared his home with Merrylegs and Ginger?

5. Which film is about the Battle of Mogadishu, also known as the Day of the Rangers, after the elite group of US soldiers who were involved in the operation?

6. Which song was a number one hit recorded by Australian rock band Men at Work. It was originally released in 1980 as the B-side to their first local single titled *Keypunch*?

7. Captain Nemo was captain of the Nautilus submarine in which Jules Verne novel?

8. What is the largest sea in the world?

9. In which Disney film did Uncle Remus tell tales about Brer Rabbit?

10. What is the title of the national anthem of Ireland?

WHODUNNIT QUEEN ANSWERS

1. TORQUAY
2. JANE
3. THE MOUSETRAP
4. HERCULE POIROT
5. THE DETECTION CLUB
6. 12
7. OXFORDSHIRE
8. PHARMACY DISPENSER
9. ST MARY MEAD
10. ALBERT FINNEY

Answer 10

CONTINUITY ANSWERS

1. LONDON BRIDGE
2. AN AMERICAN WEREWOLF IN LONDON
3. AMERICAN BEAUTY
4. BLACK BEAUTY
5. BLACK HAWK DOWN
6. DOWN UNDER
7. 20,000 LEAGUES UNDER THE SEA
8. SOUTH CHINA SEA
9. SONG OF THE SOUTH
10. THE SOLDIERS SONG

Answer 7

RHYMING TRIVIA

Each answer rhymes with each other!

1. Upon which London street does the Vaudeville Theatre stand?

2. By what alternative name is the Battle of the Bighorn known?

3. Approximately a third of which country lies within the Arctic Circle?

4. What system of writing was invented by Isaac Pitman in 1837?

5. What sports programme broadcast between 1958 and 2007 was hosted by, amongst others, Frank Bough, Des Lynam and Steve Rider?

6. What was the former name of Tasmania?

7. What consists of three sections called the anterior lobe,intermediate lobe and the posterior lobe?

8. Which woman from Wells, Somerset won a gold medal in the long jump at the 1964 Olympic Games?

9. Which river forms the border between Mexico and the US?

10. Which comedian moved from psychiatric nursing to alternative comedy, writing, presenting and acting?

IN THE KNOW

Each answer starts with 'IN'

1. What song by Elvis Presley reached number 2 in 1969?

2. What name is given to an oblong bar of gold?

3. What Glenn Miller tune did Peter Sellers request for his own funeral?

4. Glasgow Celtic won the 1967 European Cup. Who did they beat in the final?

5. What name is given to soldiers that march and manoeuvre on foot?

6. What are the front teeth between the canines called?

7. What deadly pandemic, lasted about 15 months from spring 1918?

8. What word meaning 'to make angry' and is also the name of a gum that gives off a sweet aroma when burned?

9. What does the Latin phrase 'bona fide' literally mean?

10. What song by the British rock band Queen, written by Freddie Mercury and Roger Taylor reached number one in 1981?

RHYMING TRIVIA ANSWERS

1. THE STRAND
2. CUSTER'S LAST STAND
3. FINLAND
4. SHORTHAND
5. GRANDSTAND
6. VAN DIEMEN'S LAND
7. PITUITARY GLAND
8. MARY RAND
9. RIO GRANDE
10. JO BRAND

Answer 8

IN THE KNOW ANSWERS

1. IN THE GHETTO
2. INGOT
3. IN THE MOOD
4. INTER MILAN
5. INFANTRY
6. INCISORS
7. INFLUENZA
8. INCENSE
9. IN GOOD FAITH
10. INNUENDO

Answer 2

AERIAL PHENOMENA

All answers begin with U,F or O

1. What word represents F in the phonetic alphabet?

2. What is Europe's second largest country?

3. What does a camel store in its jump?

4. What is Chopin's Piano Sonata in B Flat also known as?

5. What planet was discovered by William Herschel in 1781?

6. What nickname was given to the prohibition crime fighters led by Eliot Ness?

7. What is the fastest creature on two legs?

8. Code name was given to the 1944 operation that saw D-Day landings on Normandy beaches?

9. What is the national cheese of Greece?

10. The Old Man of Borneo is a nickname given to which animal?

A LIST OF PUBLIC JOHNS

All questions involve a John

1. Who played the Elephant Man in the 1980 film?

2. Who was shot four times and assassinated outside the Dakota in New York in 1980?

3. Who play R in the James Bond movie *The World Is Not Enough*?

4. Who wrote the novel The 39 Steps?

5. Which singer has had hits including *All Of Me*, *Happy Xmas (War is Over)* and *Ordinary People*?

6. Who wrote and portrayed Basil Fawlty?

7. Who was the second president of the USA?

8. Who became Prime Minister of the UK in 1990?

9. Which artist was born in East Bergholt in Suffolk in 1776?

10. Who became known as the Father of Television?

AERIAL PHENOMENA ANSWERS

1. FOXTROT

2. UKRAINE

3. FAT

4. FUNERAL MARCH

5. URANUS

6. UNTOUCHABLES

7. OSTRICH

Answer 7

8. OVERLORD

9. FETA

10. ORANG-UTAN

???

A LIST OF PUBLIC JOHNS ANSWERS

1. JOHN HURT
2. JOHN LENNON
3. JOHN CLEESE
4. JOHN BUCHAN
5. JOHN LEGEND
6. JOHN CLEESE (AGAIN!)
7. JOHN ADAMS
8. JOHN MAJOR
9. JOHN CONSTABLE
10. JOHN LOGIE BAIRD

Answer 3…….

And Answer 6

POETRY IN MOTION

All the 10 answers rhyme!

1. What did Sir Humphry Davy invent in 1816?

2. What was the name of the bulky umbrella carrying lady in *Martin Chuzzlewitt*?

3. At which stadium do FC Barcelona play their home matches?

4. By what affectionate nickname was Florence Nightingale known?

5. In which Disney film will you find Trusty, Pedro, Jock and Fluffy?

6. What is the more familiar name for Scrivener's Palsy?

7. A Penny Black was the world's first - what?

8. Which rock band had hits in the late 1970s with *The Logical Song* and *Breakfast In America*?

9. What name is given to a mixture of methane and other flammable gases resulting from decomposition of coal?

10. What is a more familiar term for a spreading mass of mycelium?

I'M 'ENERY THE EIGHTH

1. In what year was Henry VIII born? A) 1431 B) 1461 C) 1491

2. Who was Henry VIII's last wife?

3. How old was Henry when he ascended to the throne?

4. In which year did Henry VIII have three wives? A) 1532 B) 1534 C) 1536

5. To which Royal House did Henry belong?

6. Which of Henry's wives outlived him by a year and 8 months?

7. Who played Henry VIII in the 1971 film *Carry on Henry*?

8. Who succeeded Henry VIII to the throne?

9. Who was the only Queen to bear Henry a son?

10. True or False? Henry increased the size of the Royal Navy by 10 times.

POETRY IN MOTION ANSWERS

1. THE MINER'S SAFETY LAMP
2. SARAH GAMP
3. NOU CAMP
4. LADY WITH THE LAMP
5. LADY AND THE TRAMP
6. WRITER'S CRAMP
7. STAMP
8. SUPERTRAMP
9. FIREDAMP
10. RISING DAMP

Answer 4

I'M 'ENERY THE EIGHTH ANSWERS

1. C) 1491
2. CATHERINE PARR
3. 17
4. C) 1536
5. THE HOUSE OF TUDOR
6. CATHERINE PARR
7. SID JAMES

8. EDWARD VI
9. JANE SEYMOUR
10. TRUE

YABBA-DABBA-DOO!

1. What is the name of the Flintstones' daughter?

2. What was Wilma Flintstone's maiden name?

3. On what street do the Flintstones live?

4. Where does Fred work?

5. Who played Betty Rubble in the 1994 film *The Flintstones*?

6. What is the name of the Rubbles' baby son?

7. In a short pilot film The Flintstoines were called - what?

8. Yabba-Dabba-Doo was inspired by an advert for which product?

9. What is Fred and Barney'e favourite sport?

10. What is the name of The Flintstones' prehistoric family pet?

YOU WEAR IT WELL

1. As a solo artist, Stewart was inducted into the US Rock and Roll Hall of Fame in which year?

2. What instrument did urban legend claim that Rod played on Millie's *My Boy Lollipop* in 1964?

3. What is Rod an abbreviation for in his name?

4. What stretch of water did Rod cross according to the title of a 1975 album?

5. What Beatles hit did Rod cover in 1976?

6. In which year did Rod marry Penny Lancaster?

7. In 1990 Rod duetted on a No 5 hit of a cover version for a Pepsi ad with which female singer?

8. Which band did Rod front on *Stay With Me* in 1971?

9. With which country's football squad did Rod record *Ole Ola* in 1978?

10. Which Rod Stewart song includes the lyrics 'It's late September and I really should be back at school'?

YABBA-DABBA-DOO ANSWERS

1. PEBBLES

2. WILMA SLAGHOOPLE

3. STONE CAVE ROAD

4. ROCK HEAD AND QUARRY CAVE CONSTRUCTION COMPANY

5. ROSIE O'DONNELL

6. BAM BAM

7. THE FLAGSTONES

8. BRYLCREEM ("A little dab'll do ya")

9. TEN-PIN BOWLING

10. DINO

Answer 9

YOU WEAR IT WELL ANSWERS

1. 1994

2. HARMONICA

3. RODERICK

4. ATLANTIC (ATLANTIC CROSSING)

5. GET BACK

6. 2007

7. TINA TURNER

8. THE FACES

9. SCOTLAND

10. MAGGIE MAY

THEOLOGICAL THESPIANS

Identify the actors playing religious roles and name the film / TV show

5-4-3-2-1

How many clues do you need to identify the pop group

1. 5 POINT CLUE. This group first performed together under the name Festfolk.
2. 4 POINT CLUE. They last toured together in 1980. They released a Greatest Hits album in 1993.
3. 3 POINT CLUE. In 1974 they were triumphant in the Eurovision Contest.
4. 2 POINT CLUE. They have topped the charts all over the world with songs like *Fernando*.
5. 1 POINT CLUE. The names of this Swedish foursome are Bjorn, Benny, Agnetha and Ani-Frid.

THEOLOGICAL THESPIANS ANSWERS

1. AUDREY HEPBURN
THE NUN'S STORY 1959

2. DICK EMERY
THE DICK EMERY SHOW 1963-1981

3. JAMES NORTON
GRANTCHESTER

4. RICHARD BURTON
BECKET 1964

5. MAGGIE SMITH
SISTER ACT 1992

6. ROWAN ATKINSON
FOUR WEDDINGS AND A FUNERAL 1994

7. JENNIFER SAUNDERS
GRANDPA'S GREAT ESCAPE 2018

8. JULIE ANDREWS
THE SOUND OF MUSIC 1965

9. SEAN CONNERY
THE NAME OF THE ROSE 1986

10. SEAN BEAN
BROKEN 2017

5-4-3-2-1 ANSWER

ABBA

LUCKY DIP (3)

1. Created by Steven Knight which BBC series follows the criminal exploits of the Shelby family?

2. What is the currency of the Falkland Islands?

3. Which Rugby Union trophy was made by using recycled Indian rupees?

4. Which entertainer is portrayed by Michael Dougles in the 2013 biopic *Behind the Candelabra?*

5. In which county is Melton Mowbray, the town famous for its pork pies?

6. In which country was Bonnie Prince Charlie born?

7. For what type of traffic was the 3 miles long (5029 m) Standedge Tunnel in Yorkshire built?

8. What does a gynophobe fear?

9. Approximately what percentage of the world's population lives in Asia?

10. On to the embankment of which British motorway did a British Midland jet crash in 1989, killing 47 and seriously injuring 74 people?

THE FINAL COUNTDOWN

A final set of teasers to round off the book

1. Who is Jorge Mario Bergoglio?

2. The national flag of Cuba consists of how many alternating stripes?

3. Which battle fought on 6 July 1685, took place near Bridgwater in Somerset?

4. How many times does the number 7 appear in the numbers 1 to 100?

5. Which character in TV's Only Fools and Horses, wore a Trilby hat and was always boasting about some imagined business success?

6. 'They're tasty tasty very very tasty, they're very tasty' was the TV advertising jingle for which product?

7. Jonas Salk discovered and developed a vaccine for which disease?

8. In 1849, Elizabeth Blackwell became the first female _______?

9. What toy was introduced in Australian stores in 1957 after proving to be a popular exercise tool in schools? A) Hula Hoop B) Frisbee C) Skipping Rope D) Roller Skates

10. Although he and his wife were too afraid to use it, US President Benjamin Harrison was the first to install what in the White House?

LUCKY DIP (3) ANSWERS

1. PEAKY BLINDERS

2. FALKLAND ISLANDS POUND

3. THE CALCUTTA CUP

4. LIBERACE

5. LEICESTERSHIRE

6. ITALY

7. BOATS *(IT IS A CANAL TUNNEL)*

8. WOMEN

9. 60% *(AS AT JAN 2020)*

10. M1 *(AT KEGWORTH)*

FINAL COUNTDOWN ANSWERS

1. POPE FRANCIS *(Born Flores, Buenos Aires 17 December 1936)*

2. FIVE

3. BATTLE OF SEDGEMOOR

Answer 2

4. 20 *(7, 17, 27, 37, 47, 57, 67, 70, 71, 72, 73, 74, 75, 76, 77, 78, 79, 87, 97)*

5. MICKEY PEARCE

6. KELLOGG'S BRAN FLAKES

7. POLIO

8. DOCTOR

9. A) HULA HOOP

10. ELECTRICITY *(an engineer brought in every day to switch lights off and on)*

We hope that you have enjoyed
the quizzes in this book

Chris & Mike

Printed in Great Britain
by Amazon

42496107R00113